The Thirteen Colonies

Primary Sources

Melinda Allman, *Editor*

Lucent Books, Inc.

10911 Techn   SANTA CLARA COUNTY LIBRARY   ornia 92127

On Cover: Spirit of '76, The Colonists Going Off to Fight the
British Dunsmore, John Edward 1856–1945 American

Cover Photo: © SuperStock
© Bettmann/CORBIS, 29, 34, 58
© CORBIS, 87
Hulton/Archive by Getty Images, 12, 15, 75, 76, 81, 92
Library of Congress, 7, 48, 70, 95
© Frank G. Mayer/CORBIS, 41

Library of Congress Cataloging-in-Publication Data

Allman, Melinda
     Primary Sources / ed. Melinda Allman
         p. cm. — (The thirteen colonies)
Includes bibliographical references (p.) and index.
     Summary: A compilation of articles recalling settlement of the
thirteen colonies beginning with their origins, to forming the colonies,
life in the colonies, the fight for independence, and finally the emergence
of a new nation.
     ISBN 1-59018-011-9

Copyright 2002 by Lucent Books, Inc.
10911 Technology Place, San Diego, California 92127

Printed in the U.S.A.

Contents

Timeline

1607
John Smith and company found Jamestown, Virginia.

1635
Thomas Hooker and sixty followers found Hartford, the first permanent settlement in Connecticut.

1606
English receive permission from King James I to establish colonies in the New World.

1634
The second Lord Baltimore founds Maryland

1636
Roger Willian founds Provid in Rho Island.

1585
More than 100 colonists established the first Roanoke colony off the coast of present-day North Carolina.

1630
The Puritans found the Massachusetts Bay Colony.

1510   **1550**   **1590**   **1630**

1539
Hernando de Soto and 6000 men explore the region that will become the southwest United States.

1638
Anne Hutchinson founds the second settlement in Rhode Island; Swedish colonists arrive in Delaware.

1624
Dutch colonists arrive in New York and New Jers England's King James I takes control of the Virgi colony and makes it a royal settlement.

1609
English navigator Henry Hudson explores the Chesapeake and Delaware Bays and the Hudson River.

1623
English traders and fisherman establish settlements in New Hampshire.

1620
The Puritans leave England aboard the *Mayflower*, arrive in Cape Cod harbor, and foun the settlement of Plymouth, Massachusetts.

1492
Italian sea captain Christopher Columbus arrives in the Caribbean.

1619
The Virginia House of Burgesses, the first elected legislature in the colonies, meets for the first time; a Dutch ship brings the first African slaves to Jamestown.

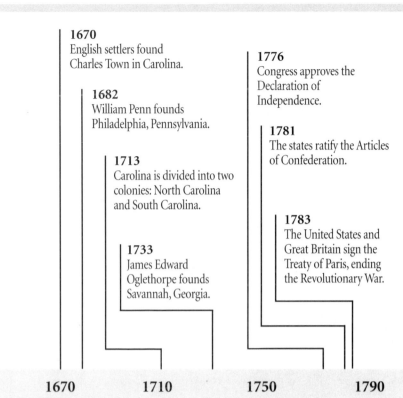

1670
English settlers found
Charles Town in Carolina.

1682
William Penn founds
Philadelphia, Pennsylvania.

1713
Carolina is divided into two
colonies: North Carolina
and South Carolina.

1733
James Edward
Oglethorpe founds
Savannah, Georgia.

1776
Congress approves the
Declaration of
Independence.

1781
The states ratify the Articles
of Confederation.

1783
The United States and
Great Britain sign the
Treaty of Paris, ending
the Revolutionary War.

1670   1710   1750   1790

1775
First shots of the American Revolution
are fired in Massachusetts; George
Washington assumes control of the
Continental forces.

1787
The Constitutional Convention opens
in Philadelphia, Pennsylvania.

1789
First meeting of the United States
Congress; George Washington is in-
augurated as the first president; the
Bill of Rights is ratified.

1786–1787
Discontented farmers
stage Shays's Rebellion in
Massachusetts.

1788
New Hampshire becomes
the first state to ratify the
Constitution; the Constitution
takes effect.

1790
Rhode Island becomes the last of
the original thirteen colonies to
sign the Constitution.

Chapter One

The Colonies' Origins

Settlement and colonization of the New World began with Christopher Columbus's arrival in 1492. Although Columbus viewed his discovery as a failure (he had been searching for a sea route to Asia), Spanish and, soon, English monarchs saw it as an opportunity, the chance to colonize and reap the monetary benefits of a vast and unsettled (so they thought) land. By the sixteenth century, explorers such as John Cabot and Hernando de Soto had landed on North American soil and established outposts that beckoned their countrymen back in Europe.

Although the Spanish remained dominant in North and South America until the late sixteenth century, the English tried repeatedly to establish a presence in the New World. During the late 1500s, they made several attempts to set up a colony called Roanoke, in present-day North Carolina. The colony failed each time, even vanishing by 1591, but the English were not deterred; they would try again.

In 1604, investors from the Virginia Company of London gained permission to explore and colonize the land along the Atlantic coast from the Cape Fear River in North Carolina to present-day Bangor, Maine. The expansive territory was then divided into two colonies: the northern colony, called Plymouth, and the southern colony, called

Virginia. Two years later, in December 1606, Captain John Smith, who would become the leader of the new southern colony, and a ship full of men left England for Virginia. They arrived on Virginia's shore four months later and established a settlement along the present-day James River. Claiming the land in the name of England's King James I, they called their settlement Jamestown.

Meanwhile, a religious revolution was taking place in England. Critics of the Church of England, who became known as Puritans, felt they needed to separate from the church in order to achieve religious salvation. Separation, though, was a crime against the state, so the Puritans decided to leave the country. In September 1620, they chartered a ship, the *Mayflower*, and set sail for the New World. They arrived in Cape Cod harbor, off the coast of Massachusetts, two months later.

The first years in Jamestown and in Massachusetts were difficult. Harsh winters, lack of food, and interaction with sometimes-hostile native tribes were problems the settlers had not anticipated. However, they forged ahead, building shelters, cultivating crops, and establishing

Claiming the land for England's King James I, Captain John Smith and the colonists named their settlement Jamestown.

relationships and alliances with their Indian neighbors. Thus, by the mid–seventeenth century, the English had claimed much of the land that would become America's thirteen colonies.

Da Verrazano Meets the Indians

Born in 1485 in Italy, Giovanni da Verrazano was one of the first Europeans to explore North America's eastern coastline. During his 1524 expedition, da Verrazano encountered a group of Native Americans off the coast of present-day Cape Fear, North Carolina. In a letter to King François I of France, da Verrazano described the meeting and the people.

Captain John de Verrazzano [Giovanni da Verrazano] to His Most Serene Majesty, the King of France, Writes:

[Around January 18, 1524] we reached a new country, which had never before been seen by any one, either in ancient or modern times. ... we perceived, by the great fires near the coast, that it was inhabited ... we drew in with the land and sent a boat on shore. Many people who were seen coming to the seaside fled at our approach, but occasionally stopping, they looked back upon us with astonishment, and some were at length induced, by various friendly signs, to come to us. These showed the greatest delight on beholding us, wondering at our dress, countenances and complexion. They then showed us by signs where we could more conveniently secure our boat, and offered us some of their provisions. That your Majesty may know all that we learned, while on shore, of their manners and customs of life, I will relate what we saw as briefly as possible. They go entirely naked, except that about the loins they wear skins of small animals like martens [carnivorous animals related to the weasel] fastened with a girdle of plaited grass [a type of belt made with braided grass], to which they tie, all around the body, the tails of other animals hanging down to the knees; all other parts of the body and the head are naked. Some wear garments similar to birds' feathers.

The complexion of these people is black, not much different from that of the Ethiopians; their hair is black and thick, and not very long, it is worn tied back upon the head in the form of a little tail. In person they are of good proportions, of middle stature, a little above our own, broad across the breast, strong in arms, and well formed in the legs and other parts of the body; the only exception to their good looks is that they have broad faces, but not all, however, as we saw many that had sharp ones, with large black eyes and a fixed expression. They are not very strong in body, but acute in mind, active and swift of foot, as far as we could judge by observation. In these last two particulars they resemble the people of the east [Asia], especially those the most remote. We could not learn a great many particulars of their usages on account of our short stay among them, and the distance of ship from the shore.

Emory Elliot, ed., *American Literature: A Prentice Hall Anthology*. Englewood Cliffs, NJ: Prentice-Hall, 1991, pp. 48–49.

The Lost Colony of Roanoke

After spending three years away from the Roanoke colony, John White, an English artist, returned in 1590 and found the area deserted. Although no one knows for sure what happened to the colonists at Roanoke (some modern scientists speculate that they were driven out by a severe drought), here, White proposes that the settlement was attacked and destroyed by Indians.

August 17 . . . we espied [spied] toward the north end of the island the light of a great fire through the woods, to which we presently rode. When we came right over against it, we let fall our grapnel [anchor] near the shore and sounded with a trumpet a call, and afterwards many familiar English tunes of songs, and called to them friendly. But we had no answer. We therefore landed at daybreak, and coming to the fire, we found the grass and sundry [numerous] rotten trees burned about the place. . . .

In all this way we saw in the sand the print of the savages' feet of two or three sorts trodden the night, and as we entered up the sandy bank, upon a tree, in the very brow thereof, were curiously carved these fair Roman letters CRO; which letters presently we knew to signify the place where I should find the planters seated, according to a secret token agreed upon between them and me at my last departure from them, which was that they should not fail to write or carve on the tree or posts of the doors the name of the place where they should be seated; for at my coming away they were prepared to remove from Roanoke 50 miles in the main.

Therefore at my departure from them in 1587 I willed them that if they should happen to be distressed in any of those places, that then they should carve over the letters or name a cross; but we found no such sign of distress. And having well considered of this, we passed towards the place where they were left in sundry houses, but we found the houses taken down, and the place very strongly enclosed with a high palisade [fence] of great trees . . . and one of the chief trees or posts at the right side of the entrance had the bark taken off, and five foot from the ground in fair capital letters was graven [carved] CROATOAN [the name of a local Indian tribe] without any cross or sign of distress. . . .

This could be no other but the deed of the savages our enemies.

David Colbert, ed., *Eyewitness to America*. New York: Pantheon Books, 1997, pp. 11–12.

Founding Jamestown

For the English settlers, the first years in Virginia were marked by hunger, cold, and fear of Indian attacks. In the following excerpt, Englishman John Smith (who refers to himself as Captain John Smith or Captain Smith throughout) describes the efforts to organize a colony at Jamestown and the meeting and attack of a nearby Native American tribe.

Captain Bartholomew Gosnoll [the leader of the Jamestown expedition], one of the first movers of this plantation [colonial settlement], having many years solicited many of his friends, but found small assistants; at last prevailed with some gentlemen, as Captain John Smith, Master Edward-Maria Wingfield, Master Robert Hunt, and many others, who depended a year upon his projects, but nothing could be effected, till by their great charge and industries it came to be apprehended [learned about] by certain of the nobility, gentry, and merchants, so that his Majesty by his letters patents, gave commission for establishing councils, to direct here [Virginia]; and to govern, and to execute there [England]. To effect this, was spent another year, and by that, three ships were provided, one of 100 tons, another of 40, and a pinnace of 20. The transportation of the company was committed to Captain Christopher Newport, a mariner well practiced for [familiar with] the western parts of America. But their orders for government were put in a box, not to be opened, nor the governors known until they arrived in Virginia.

The first land they made they called Cape Henry; where thirty of them recreating [refreshing] themselves on shore, were assaulted by five savages [Native Americans], who hurt two of the English very dangerously.

That night was the box opened, and the orders read, in which [settlers] Bartholomew Gosnoll, John Smith, Edward Wingfield, Christopher Newport, John Ratliffe, John Martin, and George Kendall, were named to be the Council, and to choose a President amongst them for a year, who with the Council should govern. Matters of moment [importance] were to be examined by a jury, but determined by the major part of the Council, in which the President had two voices [votes].

Until the 13 of May they sought a place to plant in; then the Council was sworn, Master Wingfield was chosen President, and an oration made, why Captain Smith was not admitted of the Council as the rest.

Now fell every man to work, the Council contrive [planned and built] the Fort, the rest cut down trees to make a place to pitch their tents; some provide clapboard to relade [reload] the ships, some make gardens, some nets, etc. The savages often visited us kindly. The President's overweening jealousy would admit no exercise at arms [training with weapons], or fortification but the boughs of trees cast together in the form of a half moon by the extraordinary pains and diligence of Captain Kendall.

Newport, Smith, and twenty others, were sent to discover the head of the river: by divers [various] small habitants they passed, in six days they arrived at a town called Powhatan, consisting of some twelve houses, pleasantly seated on a hill; before it three fertile isles, about it many of their cornfields, the place is very pleasant, and strong by nature, of this place the Prince is called Powhatan, and his people Powhatans. To this place the river is navigable: but higher within a mile, by reason of the rocks and Isles, there is not passage for a small

In settling Jamestown, the men had to carve a fort, gardens, and provisions out of the wilderness.

boat, this they call The Falls. The people in all parts kindly entreated them, till being returned within twenty miles of James town, they gave just cause of jealousy [vigilance, excessive guarding of]: but had God not blessed the discoverers otherwise than those at the Fort, there had been an end of that plantation; for at the Fort, where they arrived the next day, they found 17 men hurt, and a boy slain by the savages, and had it not chanced a cross barre shot from the Ships struck down a bough from a tree amongst them, that caused them to retire, our men would have all been slain since they were all at work and their arms were stored away.

Hereupon the President was contented the Fort should be palisaded [fenced], the ordnance [military supplies] mounted, his men armed and exercised: for many were the assaults, and ambushes of the savages, and our men by their disorderly straggling [scattering] were often hurt, when the savages by the nimbleness of their heels well escaped.

David Colbert, ed., *Eyewitness to America*. New York: Pantheon Books, 1997, pp. 16–17.

The First Year at Jamestown

George Percy, who later became president of the Jamestown council, sailed on an early voyage to the Virginia colony and recorded the details of that trip, the landing, and life in the New World. Below is Percy's account of the settlers' first year at Jamestown.

The 15th day of June we had built and finished our fort, which was triangle-wise, having three bulwarks [strong walks] at every corner like a half moon, and four or five pieces of artillery mounted in them. We had made ourselves sufficiently strong for these savages. We had also sown most of our corn on two mountains. . . .

Monday, the two and twentieth of June . . . Captain Newport . . . departed from James Fort for England . . . leaving us very bare and scanty of victuals [food] . . . and in danger of the savages. . . .

Our men were destroyed with cruel diseases as swellings, fluxes, burning fevers, and by wars, and some departed [died] suddenly, but for the most part they died of mere famine. There were never Englishmen left in a foreign country in such misery as we were in this new-discovered Virginia. . . . Our food was but a small can of barley sod [boiled or soaked] in water to five men a day, our drink cold water taken out of the river, which was at a flood very salt[y], at a low tide full of slime and filth, which was the destruction of many of our men. Thus we lived for . . . five months in this miserable distress, not having five able men to man our bulwarks upon any occasion. . . . Our men night and day groaning in every corner of the fort most pitiful to hear. If there were any conscience in men, it would make their hearts to bleed to hear the . . . outcries of our sick men without relief every night and day . . . some departing out of the world, many times three or four in a night; in the mornings their bodies trailed out of their cabins like dogs to be buried.

David Hawke, ed., U.S. Colonial History: Readings and Documents. New York: Bobbs-Merrill, 1966.

"I . . . exhort you to peaceable councils"

A powerful leader, the Native American chief Powhatan was, predominantly, friendly toward the English settlers, even though the colonists remained ready to fight his tribe. In this speech, delivered to Englishman John Smith in 1609, Powhatan refers to his people's friendly attitude and urges the Jamestown settlers to lay down their weapons.

I am now grown old, and must soon die; and the succession must descend, in order, to my brothers, Opitchapan, Opekankanough, and Catataugh, and then to my two sisters, and their two daughters. I wish their experience was equal to mine; and that your love to us might not be less than ours to you. Why should you take by force that from us which you can have by love? Why should you destroy us, who have provided you with food? What can you get by war? We can hide our provisions, and fly into the woods; and then you must consequently famish by wronging your friends. What is the cause of your jealousy? You see us unarmed, and willing to supply your wants, if you will come in a friendly manner, and not with swords and guns, as to invade on an enemy. I am not so simple, as not to know it is better to eat good meat, lie well, and sleep quietly with my women and children; to laugh and be merry with the English; and, being their friend, to have copper, hatchets, and whatever else I want, than to fly from all, to lie cold in the woods, feed upon acorns, roots, and such trash, and to be so hunted, that I cannot rest, eat, or sleep. In such circumstances, my men must watch, and if a twig should but break, all would cry out, "Here comes Capt. Smith"; and so, in this miserable manner, to end my miserable life; and, Capt. Smith, this might be soon your fate too, through your rashness and unadvisedness. I, therefore, exhort [urge] you to peaceable councils; and, above all, I insist that the guns and swords, the cause of all our jealousy and uneasiness, be removed and sent away.

Emory Elliot, ed., *American Literature: A Prentice Hall Anthology*. Englewood Cliffs, NJ: Prentice-Hall, 1991, pp. 58–59.

Pocahontas Rescues John Smith

One of America's most often-told legends recounts the story of Englishman John Smith and the young Indian woman Pocahontas. Although historians debate the validity of many Smith/Pocahontas stories, they generally agree that the two did meet, probably when John

With clubs raised above John Smith's head, Pocahontas lay across Smith's body, saving his life.

Smith was captured by members of Pocahontas's tribe. Here, Smith describes the scene as he is brought before Powhatan, the tribal chief and Pocahontas's father, and claims that the girl saved him from certain death.

At his [Smith's] entrance before the king, all the people gave a great shout. The queen of Appamatuck was appointed to bring him water to wash his hands, and another brought him a bunch of feathers, instead of a towel to dry them. Having feasted him after their best barbarous [uncivilized] manner they could, a long consultation was held but the conclusion was, two great stones were brought before Powhatan: then as many as could laid hands on him, dragged him to them, and thereon laid his head, and being ready with their clubs to beat out his brains, Pocahontas, the king's dearest daughter, when no entreaty [pleading] could prevail, got his head in her arms, and laid her own upon his to save him from death: whereat the emperor was contented he should live.

David Colbert, ed., *Eyewitness to America*. New York: Pantheon Books, 1997, pp.17–18.

"A rude, barbarous, and naked people"

The early settlers at Jamestown, Virginia, benefited from a precarious alliance formed between Native American leader Powhatan and English settler John Smith. After Powhatan's death, however, his brother, Opekankanough (Opachankano) became the new leader of the Powhatan Confederacy and was less willing to negotiate peaceful relations with the colonists. The continual seizure of Indian lands, primarily lands already cleared for farming, prompted Opekankanough and his tribe to attack the settlement in 1622. This assault, one of the first and most violent in the colony's history, frightened and outraged members of the Virginia Company of London, the organization that had sponsored the Jamestown settlement. In the following excerpt, officials from the Virginia Company of London argue that the 1622 attack revealed the Indians to be a treacherous people and that conquering them and their land would be beneficial to the colony.

That all men may see the impartial ingenuity of this discourse, we freely confess, that the country is not so good, as the natives are bad, whose barbarous selves need more cultivation than the ground itself, being more overspread with incivility and treachery, than that with briars. For the land, being tilled and used well by us, deceive not our expectation but rather exceeded it far, being so thankful as to return a hundred for one. But the savages, though never a nation used so kindly upon so small desert, have instead of that harvest which our pains merited, returned nothing but briars and thorns, pricking even to death many of their benefactors. Yet doubt we not, but that as all wickedness is crafty to undo itself, so these also have more wounded themselves than us, God Almighty making way for severity there, where a fair gentleness would not take place. The occasion whereof thus I relate from thence.

The last May [1622] there came a letter from Sir Francis Wiat [Wyatt] Governor in Virginia, which did advertise that when in November last [1621] he arrived in Virginia and entered upon his government, he found the country settled in a peace (as all men there thought), sure and unviolable, not only because it was solemnly ratified and sworn, but as being advantageous to both parts; to the savages as the weaker, under which they were safely sheltered and defended; to us, as being the easiest way then thought to pursue and advance our projects of buildings, plantings, and effecting their conversion by peaceable and fair means. And such was the conceit [conception] of firm peace and amity [friendship] as that there was seldom or never a sword worn.... The plantations of particular adventurers and planters were placed scatteringly and straggingly [scattered] as a choice vein of rich ground invited them, and the further from neighbors held the better. The houses generally set open to the savages, who were always friendly entertained at the tables of the English, and commonly lodged in their bedchambers. The old planters (as they thought now come to reap the benefit of their long travels) placed with wonderful content upon their private lands, and their familiarity with the natives, seeming to open a fair gate for their conversion to Christianity.

The country being in this estate, an occasion was ministered of sending to Opachankano, the King of these savages, about the middle of March last, what time the messenger returned back with these words from him, that he held the peace concluded so firm as the sky should sooner fall than it dissolve. Yea, such was the treacherous dissimulation of that people who then had contrived our destruction, that even two days before the massacre, some of our men were guided through the woods by them in safety. . . . Yea, they borrowed our own boats to convey themselves across the river (on the banks of both sides whereof all our plantations were) to consult of the devilish murder that ensued, and of our utter extirpation [complete destruction], which God of His mercy (by the means of themselves converted to Christianity) prevented. And as well on the Friday morning (the fatal day) the twenty-second of March, as also in the evening, as on other days before, they came unarmed into our houses, without bows or arrows, or other weapons, with deer, turkey, fish, fur, and other provisions to sell and trade with us for glass, beads, and, other trifles. Yet in some places, they sat down at breakfast with our people at their tables, whom immediately with their own tools and weapons either laid down, or standing in their houses, they basely and barbarously murdered, not sparing either age or sex, man, woman, or child, so sudden in their cruel execution that few or none discerned the weapon or blow that brought them to destruction. In which manner they also slew many of our people then at their several work and husbandries [agriculture] in the fields, and without their houses, some in planting corn and tobacco, some in gardening, some in making brick, building, sawing, and other kinds of husbandry, they well knowing in what places and quarters each of our men were, in regard of their daily familiarity and resort to us for trading and other negotiations, which the more willingly was by us continued and cherished for the desire we had of effecting that great masterpiece of works, their conversion. And by this means that fatal Friday morning, there fell under the bloody and barbarous hands of that perfidious [faithless, disloyal] and inhuman people, contrary to all laws of God and men, of nature and nations, three hundred forty seven men, women, and children, most by their own weapons. And not being content with taking away life alone, they fell after again upon the dead, making as well as they could, a fresh murder, defacing, dragging, and mangling the dead carcasses into many pieces, and carrying some parts away in derision [ridiculing, scornful], with base and brutish triumph. . . .

That the slaughter had been universal, if God had not put it into the heart of an Indian belonging to one Perry to disclose it, who living in the house of one Pace, was urged by another Indian his brother (who came the night before and lay with him) to kill Pace. Telling further that by such an hour in the morning a number would come from different places to finish the execution, who failed not at the time, Perry's Indian rose out of his bed and revealed it to Pace, that used him as a son. And thus the rest of the colony that had warning given them by this means was saved. Such was (God be thanked for it) the good fruit of an infidel [one who is not a Christian] converted to Christianity. For though three hundred and more of ours died by many of these pagan infidels, yet thousands of ours were saved by the means of one of them alone which was made a Christian. Blessed be God forever, whose mercy endureth forever. . . .

Thus have you seen the particulars of this massacre, wherein treachery and cruelty have done their worst to us, or rather to themselves; for whose understanding is so shallow, as not to perceive that this must needs be for the good of the plantation after, and the loss of this blood to make the body more healthful, as by these reasons may be manifest [made clear, shown].

First, because betraying innocence never rests unpunished. . . .

Secondly, because our hands, which before were tied with gentleness and fair usage, are now set at liberty by the treacherous violence of the savages, not untying the knot, but cutting it. So that we, who hitherto have had possession of no more ground than their waste, and our purchase at a valuable consideration to their own contentment gained, may now, by right of war and law of nations, invade the country, and destroy them who sought to destroy us. Whereby we shall enjoy their cultivated places, possessing the fruits of others' labors. Now their cleared grounds in all their villages (which are situated in the fruitfulest places of the land) shall be inhabited by us, whereas heretofore the grubbing of woods was the greatest labor.

Thirdly, because those commodities which the Indians enjoyed as much or rather more than we, shall now also be entirely possessed by us. The deer and other beasts will be in safety, and infinitely increase, which heretofore not only in the general huntings of the King, but by each particular Indian were destroyed at all times of the year, without any difference of male, dame, or young.

There will be also a great increase of wild turkeys, and other weighty fowl, for the Indians never put difference of destroying the hen, but kill them whether in season or not, whether in breeding time, or sitting on their eggs, or having new hatched, it is all one to them. . . .

Fourthly, because the way of conquering them is much more easy than of civilizing them by fair means, for they are a rude, barbarous, and naked people, scattered in small companies, which are helps to victory, but hindrance to civility. Besides that, a conquest may be of many, and at once; but civility is in particular and slow, the effect of long time, and great industry. Moreover, victory of them may be gained many ways: by force, by surprise, by famine in burning their corn, by destroying and burning their boats, canoes, and houses, by breaking their fishing wares, by assailing them in their huntings, whereby they get the greatest part of their sustenance in winter, by pursuing and chasing them with our horses and bloodhounds to draw after them, and mastiffs [large, powerful dogs] to tear them.

Susan Kingsbury, ed., *The Records of the Virginia Company of London*, vol. 3 (Washington, DC: GPO, 1933).

The Pilgrims' Landing and First Winter

In 1620, the Pilgrims anchored their ship, the Mayflower, off the coast of Cape Cod, Massachusetts. Soon after, they sent landing parties ashore to survey the land and appraise it for settlement. In this piece, William Bradford, who led the Pilgrims' crossing from England, describes that voyage, landing, and the first year the settlers spent in the New World.

Being thus arrived at Cape-Cod . . . they having brought a large ship with them out of England, stowed in quarters in the ship, they now got her out, and set their carpenters to work to trim her up, but being much bruised and shattered in the ship with foul weather, they saw she would be long in mending. Whereupon a few of them tendered [offered] themselves, to go by land and discover those nearest places, while the ship was in mending. . . . It was conceived there might be some danger in the attempt, yet seeing them resolute they were permitted to go, being 16 of them well armed under the conduct of Captain Standish. . . . After some hours sailing, it began to snow and rain, and about the middle of the afternoon, the wind increased, and the sea became very rough; and they broke their rudder, and it was as much as two men could do to steer her with a couple of oars. But their pilot bade them be of good cheer for he saw the harbor, but the storm increasing, and night drawing on, they bore what sail they could to get in, while they could see; but herewith they broke their mast in three pieces and their sail fell overboard, in a very high sea. . . .

But a lusty [strong] seaman which steered, bode those which rowed if they were men, about with her, or else they were all cast away; which they did with speed, so he bid them be of good cheer, and row justly for there was a fair sound before them, and he doubted not, but they should find one place or other, where they might ride in safety. And though it was very dark, and rained sore [severely], yet in the end they got under the lee [side protected from the wind] of a small island and remained there all that night in safety. . . .

But though this had been a day and night of much trouble, and danger unto them; yet God gave them a morning of comfort and refreshing (as usually he does to his children) for the next day was a fair sunshining day, and they found themselves to be on an island secure from the Indians; where they might dry their stuff, fix their pieces, and rest themselves, and gave God thanks for his mercies, in their manifold deliverances [various rescues]. And this being the last day of the week, they prepared there to keep the Sabbath; on Monday they sounded [measured the depth of] the harbor, and found it fit for shipping; and marched into the land, and found many cornfields, and little running brooks, a place (as they supposed) fit for situation [living], at least it was the best they could find, and the season, and their present necessity made them glad to accept of it. So they returned to their ship again with this news to the rest of their people, which did much comfort their hearts....

Afterwards [they] took better view of the place, and resolved where to pitch their dwelling; and the 25th day [December 25, 1620] began to erect the first house, for common use to receive them, and their goods....

But that which was most sad, and lamentable, was, that in two or three months the half of their company died, especially in January and February, being the depth of winter, and wanting houses and other comforts; being infected with the scurvy and other diseases, which this long voyage and their inaccommodate condition had brought upon them; so as there died some times two or three of a day, in the forsaid time; that of one hundred and odd persons scarce fifty remained: and of these in the time of most distress there was but six or seven sound persons; who to their great commendations, be it spoken, spared no pains, night nor day, but with abundance of toil and hazard of their own health, fetched them wood, made them fires, dressed their meat, made their beds, washed their loathsome clothes, clothed and unclothed them. In a word did all the homely, and necessary offices for them, which dainty and queasy stomachs cannot endure to hear named and all this willingly and cheerfully, without any grudging in the least, showing herein their true love unto their friends and brethren. A rare example and worthy to be remembered, two of these seven were Mr William Brewster, their Reverend Elder, and Miles Standish, their Captain and military commander, (unto whom myself, and many others were much beholden in our low, and sick condition)....

All this while the Indians came skulking about them, and would sometimes show themselves aloof [having no interest], but when any approached near them, they would run away; and once they stole away their tools when they had been at work and were gone to diner. But about the 16th of March a certain Indian came boldly amongst them, and spoke to them in broken English which they could well understand, but marveled at it; at length they understood by discourse [conversation] with him, that he was not of these parts, but belonged to the eastern parts where some English ships came to fish, with whom he was acquainted, and could name sundry [several] of them by their names, amongst whom he had got his language. He became profitable to them in acquainting them with many things concerning the state of the country in the east parts where he lived . . . of the people here, of their names, number and strength, of their situation and distance from this place, and who was chief amongst them. His [the Indian's] name was Samasett; he told them also of another Indian whose name was Squanto, a native of this place, who had been in England and could speak better English than himself. Being after some time of entertainment, and gifts dismissed, a while after he came again, and five more with him, and they brought again all the tools that were stolen away before, and made way for the coming of their great Sachem [Native American Chief], called Massasoyt. Who about four or five days after came with the chief of his friends, and other attendance with the aforesaid Squanto. With whom after friendly entertainment, and some gifts given him, they made a peace with him (which has now continued this 24 years) in these terms:

1. That neither he nor any of his, should injure or do hurt, to any of their people.
2. That if any of his, did any hurt to any of theirs; he should send the offender, that they might punish him.
3. That if any thing were taken away from any of theirs, he should cause it to be restored; and they should do the like to his.
4. If any did unjustly war against him, they would aide him; if any did war against them, he should aide them.
5. He should send to his neighbors confederates [allies] to certify them of this [treaty], that they might not wrong them [the Pilgrims], but might be likewise comprised in the conditions of peace.
6. That when [Mossasoyt's] men came to [the Pilgrims,] they should leave their bows and arrows behind them. . . .

They [the Pilgrims] began now to gather in the small harvest they had; and to fit up their houses and dwellings, against winter, being all well recovered in health and strength; and had off things in good plenty, for as some were thus employed in affairs abroad; others were exercised in fishing, about cod, and bass, other fish of which they took good store, of which every family had their portion; all the summer there was no want; and now began to come in store of fowl, as winter approached, of which this place did abound when they came first, (but afterward decreased by degrees), and besides water fowl, there was great store of wild turkeys, of which they took many, besides venison etc. Besides they had about a peck [half a bushel or two gallons] a meal a week to a person, or now since harvest, Indian corn to that proportion, which made many afterwards write so largely of their plenty here to their friends in England, which were not fained, but true reports.

David Colbert, ed., *Eyewitness to America*. New York: Pantheon Books, 1997, pp. 22–24.

The Mayflower Compact

Upon arriving in Massachusetts, William Bradford and forty Pilgrims drafted and signed the Mayflower Compact, *a document that allowed them to form and establish a government and laws.*

In the Name of God, Amen. We, whose names are underwritten, the loyal subjects of our . . . Sovereign Lord King James [of England], by the Grace of God of Great Britain, France, and Ireland King, Defender of the Faith, etc.

Having undertaken, for the Glory of God and Advancement of the Christian Faith and Honour of our King and Country, a Voyage to plant the First Colony in the Northern Parts of Virginia, do by these presents solemnly and mutually in the presence of God and one of another, Covenant and Combine ourselves together into a Civil Body Politic, for our better ordering and preservation and furtherance of the ends aforesaid; and by virtue hereof to enact, constitute and frame such just and equal Laws, Ordinances, Acts, Constitutions and Offices, from time to time, as shall be thought most meet and convenient for the general good of the Colony, unto which we promise all due submission and obedience. In witness whereof we have hereunder subscribed our names at Cape Cod [Massachusetts], the 11th of November, in the year of the reign of our Sovereign Lord King James, of England, France and Ireland the eighteenth, and of Scotland the fifty-fourth, Anno Domini [in the year] 1620.

William Bradford, *Of Plymouth Plantation, 1620–1647.* Samuel Eliot Morison, ed. New York: Knopf, 1966, pp. 75–76.

A Natural Right and a Civil Right

Some Puritans resisted leaving England for the New World, arguing that they had no right to settle lands long occupied by others. John Winthrop, a devoted Puritan who became governor of the Massachusetts colony, disagreed. Here, he explains that there is more than enough land for all.

That which lies common and hath never been replenished or subdued is free to any that will possess and improve it, for God hath given to . . . men a double right to the earth. There is a natural right and a civil right. The first right was natural when men held the earth in common. . . . And then as men and the cattle increased, they [claimed] certain parcels of ground by enclosing and peculiar manurance [occupancy]. And this in time gave them a civil right. . . . And for the natives in New England; they enclose no land, neither have any settled habitation, nor any tame cattle to improve the land by, and so have not other but a natural right to those countries. So . . . if we leave them [enough] for their use we may lawfully take the rest, there being more than enough for them and us.

David Hawke, ed., *U.S. Colonial History: Readings and Documents.* New York: Bobbs-Merrill, 1966.

Chapter Two

Forming the Colonies

As the settlers in Massachusetts and Virginia struggled to maintain their holds in the New World, colonies sprang up all along the Atlantic coastline. Although there were many reasons for these new settlements, quarrels over religion were the most prominent.

Religious differences appeared in the colonies almost immediately. The Puritans who controlled Massachusetts were a strict congregation that did not permit differing opinions. Thus, those whose beliefs strayed from the Puritans' way of thinking had three choices: They could change their beliefs, be persecuted by the Puritans, or they could leave. Many chose to leave.

In 1635, officials of the Massachusetts Bay Colony banished minister Roger Williams. Williams, whose political and religious beliefs differed from the Puritans, had criticized his English brethren for seizing lands in the New World, particularly Indian lands, without paying for them. Following his banishment, Williams traveled south, purchased land from the Indians, and, with a group of followers, established the settlement of Providence in what would become Rhode Island. Other dissenters left Massachusetts for religious reasons as well—among them, Thomas Hooker in Connecticut and William Penn in Pennsylvania.

These new colonies were not without conflict or controversy. The ever-present fear of Indian attacks remained, and as colonists pushed west from the coast, the conflicts only got worse. In 1637, the tensions escalated into war between the Massachusetts and Connecticut settlers and the Pequot Indian tribe. The Pequot War, as the conflict came to be known, resulted in the near eradication of the tribe and the formation of the New England Confederation, a collection of settlements intended to defend the colonists against Indian attacks. This confederation proved to be the earliest sign of the colonial unity that would develop a century later.

Meanwhile, other colonies were dealing with controversy. Some settlers in Massachusetts, Pennsylvania, and Georgia questioned the legality and morality of the slave trade. At the time, landowners and others throughout the colonies owned slaves and had since the first Africans arrived in Jamestown in 1619. Although some settlers called for the abolition of a business they deemed immoral, slavery ultimately remained a part of the colonies' social and industrial makeup for one simple reason—it was essential to the economy.

By the beginning of the eighteenth century, the thirteen American colonies, conflicts and all, were firmly established. The colonists were also becoming tired of English rule. The king and his laws were very far away, and the Americans, as the colonists had begun to call themselves, wanted to be independent. It became increasingly obvious that a revolution was inevitable.

A May Day Celebration

Religious differences appeared in the Massachusetts Bay Colony almost as soon as the first Puritans arrived. Such divisions ultimately led to the formation of colonies outside Massachusetts (Rhode Island and Connecticut among them). Here, Thomas Morton, an Anglican Englishman, describes a May Day celebration during which he and his followers encountered a group of Puritans, who followed strict religious codes forbidding such activities as music and dance. Morton's account provides one of the few descriptions of non-Puritan life in colonial Massachusetts.

The Inhabitants of Pasonagessit [in Massachusetts] (having translated the name of their habitation from that ancient savage name to Merry-Mount) did devise amongst themselves to have it performed in a solemn manner with revels [celebrations] and merriment after the old English custom. They prepared to set up a Maypole [decorated pole around which people dance on May Day] upon the festival day of Philip and Jacob [May Day, a Catholic holiday honoring the saints Philip and Jacob]; and brewed a barrel of excellent beer, and provided a case of bottles to be spent [consumed], with other good cheer, for all comers of that day. And because they would have it in a complete form, they had prepared a song fitting to the time and present occasion. And upon Mayday they brought the Maypole to the place appointed, with drums, guns, pistols, and other fitting instruments, for that purpose; and there erected it with the help of Savages, that came there to see the manner of our revels. A goodly pine tree, eighty feet long, was reared [erected] up, with a pair of buck's horns nailed on, somewhat near unto the top of it: where it stood as a fair sea mark [an elevated object serving as a guide for sailors] for directions; how to find out the way to my host of Merry-Mount [Morton was referring to himself].

The setting up of this Maypole was a lamentable spectacle to the precise separatists [the Pilgrims] that lived at new Plymouth. They termed it an Idol, yea they called it the Calf of Horeb [an idol falsely worshipped by the Israelites as their deliverer from slavery in Egypt], and stood at defiance with the place, naming it Mount Dagon; threatening to make it a woeful mount not a merry mount. . . .

There was likewise a merry song made, which (to make their revels more fashionable) was sung with a chorus, every man bearing his part; which they performed in a dance, hand in hand about the Maypole while one of the Company sung, and filled out the good liquor like Ganymede [a Roman god] and Jupiter [the chief Roman god]:

Drink and be merry, merry, merry, boys,
Let all your delight be in Hymen's [the Greek god of marriage] joys,
Joy to Hymen now the day is come,
About the merry Maypole take a room.
Make greene garlands, bring bottles out;
And fill sweet Nectar [in Greek and Roman myth, the drink of
the gods], freely about,

Uncover thy head, and fear no harm,
For here's good liquor to keep it warm. . . .

This harmless mirth [gladness] made by young men (that lived in hope to have wives brought over to them . . .) was much distasted by the precise Separatists . . . troubling their brains more than reason would require about things that are indifferent [unimportant] and from that time sought occasion against my honest host of Merry-Mount to overthrow his undertakings, and to destroy his plantation quite and clean [completely]. . . .

David Colbert, ed., *Eyewitness to America*. New York: Pantheon Books, 1997, pp. 25–26.

Roger Williams Banishment

In October 1635, the General Court of Massachusetts banished minister Roger Williams from the Massachusetts Bay Colony. The court disagreed with Williams's religious and political beliefs, primarily his accusation that the English didn't have the right to seize Indian lands without paying for them and the fact that his interpretations of the scriptures challenged the authority of the colonial government. Ultimately, Williams left Massachusetts and formed the colony of Rhode Island. The next year, during a trip to England, Williams found himself, once again, debating his banishment, this time with John Cotton, a Puritan minister and leader. The excerpt below, which was published in England in 1636, is Williams's answer to Cotton's allegations that the banishment was justified.

But because the Reader may ask both Mr. [John] Cotton and me, what were the grounds of such a sentence of Banishment against me, which are here called sandy, I shall relate in brief what those grounds were, some whereof he is pleased to discuss in this Letter, and others of them not to mention.

After my public trial and answers at the general Court, one of the most eminent Magistrates (whose name and speech may by others be remembered) stood up and spake:

Mr. Williams (said he) holds forth these 4 particulars; First, that we have not our land by patent from the King, but that the natives are the true owners of it, and that we ought to repent of such a receiving it by patent. Secondly, that it is not lawful to call a wicked person to swear, to pray, as being actions of Gods Worship. Thirdly, that it is not lawful to hear any of the ministers of the parish assemblies in England. Fourthly, that the civil magistrates power extends only to the bodies and goods, and outward state of men, etc.

I acknowledge the particulars were rightly summed up, and I also hope, that, as I then maintained the rocky strength of them to my own and other consciences satisfaction so (through the Lords assistance) I shall be ready for the same grounds,

Minister Roger Williams, disagreeing that the colonists had a right to seize Indian lands, was banished from the Massachusetts Bay Colony.

not only to be bound and banished, but to die also, in New England, as for most holy truths of God in Christ Jesus.

Yes but (said he) upon those grounds you banished your self from the society of the churches in these countries.

I answer, if Mr. Cotton means my own voluntary withdrawing from those churches resolved to continue in those evils, and persecuting the witnesses of the Lord presenting light unto them, I confess it was my own voluntary act; yea, I hope the act of the Lord Jesus sounding forth in me (a poor despised rams horn) the blast which shall in his own holy season cast down the strength and confidence of those inventions of men in the worshipping of the true and living God. And lastly, his act in enabling me to be faithful in any measure to suffer such great and mighty trials for his names sake. But if by banishing my self he intend the act of civil banishment from their common earth and aire, I then observe with grief the language of the dragon in a lambs lip. Among other expressions of the dragon are not these common to the witnesses of the Lord Jesus rent and torn by his persecutions? Go now, say you are persecuted, you are persecuted for

Christ, suffer for your conscience: no, it is your schisme, heresy, obstinacy, the devil hath deceived thee, thou hast justly brought this upon thee, thou hast banished thy self, etc. Instances are abundant in so many books of Martyrs, and the experience of all men, and therefore I spare to recite in so short a treatise.

Secondly, if he mean this civil act of banishing, why should he call a civil sentence from the civil State, within a few weeks execution in so sharp a time of New Englands cold. Why should he call this a banishment from the churches, except he silently confess, that the frame or constitution of their churches is but implicitly national (which yet they profess against) for otherwise why was I not yet permitted to live in the world, or commonwealth, except for this reason, that the commonwealth and church is yet but one, and he that is banished from the one, must necessarily be banished from the other also....

Mr. Cotton [said]. And yet it may be they passed that sentence against you, not upon that ground: but for ought I know, for your other corrupt Doctrines, which tend to the disturbance both of civil and holy peace, as may appear by that answer which was sent to the brethren of the Church of Salem and your self.

I answer, it is no wonder that so many having been demanded the cause of my sufferings have answered, that they could not tell for what, since Mr. Cotton himself knows not distinctly what cause to assign: but said, it may be they passed not that sentence on that ground, etc. Oh, where was the waking care of so excellent and worthy a man, to see his brother and beloved in Christ so afflicted, he knows not distinctly for what.

He alleged a scripture, to prove the sentence righteous, and yet concluded it may be it was not for that, but for other corrupt Doctrines which he named not, nor any Scripture to prove them corrupt, or the sentence righteous for that cause. O that it may please the Father of lights to awaken both himself and other of my honored countrymen, to see how though their hearts wake (in respect of personal grace and life of Jesus) yet they sleep insensible of much concerning the purity of the Lords worship, or the sorrows of such whom they call brethren, and beloved in Christ, afflicted by them.

But though he name not these corrupt doctrines, a little before I have, as they were publicly summed up and charged upon me, and yet none of them tending to the breach of holy or civil peace, of which I have ever desired to be unfainedly [sincerely] tender, acknowledging the Ordinance of Magistracie to be properly and adequately fitted by God, to preserve the civil state in civil peace and order: as he had also appointed a spiritual government and governors in matters pertaining to his worship and the consciences of men, both which governments, governors, laws, offences, punishments, are essentially distinct, and the confounding of them brings all the world into combustion. ...

Ans. However Mr. Cotton believes and writes of this point, yet has he not duly considered these following particulars:

First the faithful labors of many witnesses of Jesus Christ, extant to the world, abundantly proving, that the Church of the Jews under the Old Testament in the type, and the Church of the Christians under the New Testament in the Antitype, were both separate from the world; and that when they have opened a gap in the hedge or wall of separation between the garden of the church and the wilderness of the world, God hath ever broke down the wall it self, removed the candlestick, etc. and made his garden a wilderness, as at this day. And that therefore if he will ever please to restore his garden and paradise again, it must of necessity be walled in peculiarly unto himself from the world, and that all that shall be saved out of the world are to be transplanted out of the wilderness of world, and added unto his church or garden.

From Roger Williams, "Mr. Cotton's Letter Lately Printed, Examined, and Answered." In *Publications of the Narragansett Club*. Vol. 1. Providence, 1866.

Promoting Colonization in Maryland

In 1633, Andrew White, a Jesuit missionary, wrote the following in an effort to encourage settlement in Maryland.

This province, his most serene majesty ... in the month of June, 1632, gave to the Lord Baron of Baltimore [leader of Maryland] and his heirs forever. ... Therefore the ... Baron has resolved immediately to lead a colony into that region. ... He has ... weighed ... all the advantages and disadvantages which hitherto advanced or impeded other colonies, and found nothing which does not . . . promise . . . success. . . . Such gentlemen as shall pay down one hundred pounds . . . to convey five men . . . shall be assigned . . . two thousand acres of good land. . . .

The natural position of the [colony] is . . . advantageous. . . . The air is serene and mild, neither exposed to the burning heat of Florida or ancient Virginia, nor withered by the cold of New England, but . . . enjoys the advantages of each. . . . On the east it is washed by the ocean: on the west it adjoins an almost boundless continent. . . .

There are two . . . bays most abundant in fish . . . and noble rivers . . . where . . . trade with the Indians is so profitable that a certain merchant, the last year, shipped beaver skins at a price of forty thousand pieces of gold. . . . In the level . . . country, there is a great abundance of grass, but the region is for the most part shaded with forests; oaks and walnut trees are the most common. . . .

So great is the abundance of swine and deer that they are [more] troublesome than profitable. Cows, also, are innumerable. . . . What shall I say of the lupines [herbs], beans, garden roots . . . when even the peas . . . grow in ten days, to a height of fourteen inches. . . . There is hope, too, of finding gold; for the neighboring people wear braclets of unwrought gold and long strings of pearls.

Richard Walsh, ed., *The Mind and Spirit of Early America: Sources in American History, 1607–1789.* New York: Meredith, 1969.

The Maryland Toleration Act

Because Protestants increasingly outnumbered Catholics in Maryland, Lord Baltimore, the leader of the Maryland colony, endeavored to protect the religious freedom of Catholics. In 1649, he passed the Toleration Act, a milestone in the history of religious freedom for both Catholics and Protestants.

Whereas the enforcing of the conscience in matters of religion has frequently fallen out to be of dangerous consequence in those commonwealths where it has been practiced, and for the more quiet and peaceable government of this province, and the better to preserve mutual love and amity [friendship] among the inhabitants thereof, be it, therefore, also by the Lord Proprietary, with the advice and consent of this assembly, ordained and enacted ... that no person or persons whatsoever within this province ... professing to believe in Jesus Christ, shall from henceforth be in any way troubled, molested, or discountenanced for ... his or her religion, nor in the free exercise thereof ... nor in any way compelled to the belief or exercise of any other religion against his or her consent. ...

And that all ... that shall presume ... willfully to wrong, disturb, trouble, or molest any person whatsoever within this province professing to believe in Jesus Christ for ... his or her religion or the free exercise thereof ... that such person or persons so offending shall be compelled to pay treble [triple] damages to the party so wronged or molested. ... If the party so offending shall refuse or be unable to recompense [compensate, repay] the party so wronged, or to satisfy such fine or forfeiture, then such offender shall be severely punished by public whipping and imprisonment.

Mortimer J. Adler, ed., *The Annals of America*. Vol. I. *1493–1754*, Discovering a New World. Chicago: Encyclopedia Britannica, 1968.

Victory over the Pequots

Relations between the Native Americans and English settlers in New England deteriorated as the colonists pushed their settlements west from the coast. Tensions escalated and ultimately resulted in a bloody conflict called the Pequot War. Here, John Mason, an English leader during the war, gives an account of the Puritans' victory in that conflict.

Thus were they [the Indians] now at their wits end, who not many hours before exalted themselves in their great pride, threatening and resolving the utter ruin of all the English, exulting and rejoicing with songs and dances. But God was above them, who laughed his enemies and the enemies of his people to scorn, making them as a fiery oven. Thus were the stout-hearted spoiled, having slept their lost sleep ... Thus did the Lord judge among the heathen, filling the place with dead bodies.

And here we may see the just judgment of God, in sending (even the very night before this assault) 150 men from their other fort, to join with them of that place; who were designed—as some of themselves reported—to go forth against the English at that very instant when this heavy stroke came upon them, where they perished with their fellows. So that the mischief they intended came upon their own pate [head]. They were taken in their own snare, and we through mercy escaped. And thus in little more than an hour's space was their impregnable [impossible to capture] fort with themselves utterly destroyed, to the number of six or seven hundred, as some of themselves confessed. There were only seven taken captive and about seven escaped.

Thus the Lord was pleased to smite [destroy] our enemies in the hinder parts and to give us their land for an inheritance, who remembered us in our low estate, and redeemed us out of our enemies' hands. Let us

Settlers raid an Indian fort during the Pequot War.

therefore praise the Lord for his goodness and his wonderful works to the Children of men!

John Mason, *A Brief History of the Pequot War*. Boston, MA: S. Kneeland & T. Green, 1736, pp. 9–10, 12.

A Letter from Elizabeth Bacon

During the late seventeenth century, life in the interior parts of the colonies (those away from the coast) was particularly dangerous. Men, women, and children were subject to vicious Indian attacks, and the settlers lived in constant fear. Virginia governor William Berkeley was more sensitive to the natives than some settlers would have liked, a fact that prompted colonist Nathaniel Bacon to form a militia and organize raids against nearby tribes. In 1676, Bacon's wife, Elizabeth, wrote this letter to her sister, detailing the frightening events leading up to her husband's raids. She also expresses her contempt for Governor Berkeley, a sentiment shared by only a few of the colony's residents rather than the majority as her husband contended.

Dear Sister,

I pray God keep the worst Enemy I have from ever being in such a sad condition as I have been in . . . occasioned by the troublesome Indians, who have killed one of our Overseers [supervisors] at an outward [distant] plantation which we had, and we have lost a great stock of cattle, which we had upon it, and a good crop that we should have made there, such plantation Nobody durst [dares] come nigh [near], which is a very great loss to us.

If you had been here, it would have grieved your heart to hear the pitiful complaints of the people, The Indians killing the people daily the [Governor, William Berkeley] not taking any notice of it for to hinder [stop] them, but let them daily do all the mischief they can: I am sure if the Indians were not cowards, they might have destroyed all the upper plantations, and killed all the people upon them; the Governour so much their friend, that he would not suffer anybody to hurt one of the Indians; and the poor people came to your brother [in-law Nathaniel Bacon] to desire him to help against the Indians, and he being very much concerned for the loss of his Overseer, and for the loss of so many men and women and children's lives every day, he was willing to do them all the good he could; so he begged of the Governour for a commission [an appointment allowing him the power to form a militia] in several letters to him, that he might go out against them, but he would not grant one, so daily more mischief done by them, so your brother not able to endure any longer, he went out without a commission. The Governour being very angry with him put out high things against him, and told me that he would most certainly hang him as soon as he returned, which he would certainly have done; but what for fear of the Governour's hanging him, and what for fear of the Indians killing him brought me to this sad condition, but blessed be God he came in very well, with the loss of a very few men; never was known such a fight in Virginia with so few men's loss. The fight did continue nigh [nearly] a night and a day without any intermission. They did destroy a great many of the Indians, thanks be to God, and might have killed a great many more, but the Governour were so much the Indians' friend and our enemy, that he sent the Indians word that Mr. Bacon was out against them, that they might save themselves. After Mr. Bacon was come in he was forced to keep a guard of soldiers about his house, for the Governour would certainly have had his life taken away privately, if he would have had opportunity; but the country does so really love him, that they would not leave him alone anywhere; there was not anybody against him but the Governour and a few of his great men, which have got their Estates by the Governour; surely if your brother's crime had been so great, all the country would not have been for him, you never knew any better beloved than he is. I do verily [truly] believe that rather than he should come to any hurt by the Governour or anybody else they would most of them willingly lose their lives. The Governour has sent his Lady [wife] into England with great complaints to the King against Mr. Bacon, but when Mr. Bacon's and all the people's complaints be also heard, I hope it may be very well. Since your brother [in law] came in he hath sought to the Governour for commission, but none would be granted him, so that the Indians have had a very good time, to do more mischief. They have murdered and destroyed a great many whole families since, and the men resolving not to go under any but your brother, most of the country did rise in Arms [take up weapons], and went down to the Governour, and would not stir till he had given a commission to your brother which he has now done. He is made General of the Virginia War, and now I live in great fear, that he should lose his life amongst them. They are come very nigh our Plantation where we live.

Karen Ordahl Kupperman, ed., *Major Problems in American Colonial History*. Lexington, MA: D. C. Heath, 1993, pp. 202–205.

The Propriety of Pennsylvania

After having endured prison for his religious beliefs, William Penn, a social reformer and advocate of religious freedom, decided in 1681 to create his own colony, one that would guarantee equality and fairness for all its people. Penn decided to buy the land himself—he did not believe he had the right to seize what the Native Americans already possessed—and established the colony of Pennsylvania in 1682. To entice settlers to the area, Penn drafted The Propriety of Pennsylvania, *in which he discussed, among other things, the beauty of the land and the peaceful relationship he had with the area's natives.*

For the Province, the general condition of it take as followeth:

I. The country itself in its soil, air, water, seasons, and produce both natural and artificial is not to be despised [looked down upon]. The land containeth diverse sorts of earth.... God in his wisdom having ordered it so, that the advantages of the country are divided, the backlands being generally three to one richer than those that lie by navigable waters....

VI. Of living creatures: fish, fowl, and beasts of the woods, here are diverse sorts, some for food and profit, and some for profit only. ... The creatures for profit only by skin or fur, and that are natural to these parts, are the wild cat, panther, otter, wolf, fox, fisher, minx, muskrat; and of the water, the whale for oil, of which we have good store; and two companies of whalers, whose boats are built, will soon begin their work, which hath the appearance of a considerable improvement. To say nothing of our reasonable hopes of good cod in the bay....

XI. The Natives I shall consider in their persons, language, manners, religion, and government, with my sense of their original. For their persons, they are generally tall, straight, well-built, and of singular proportion [size]; they treat [behave] strong and clever, and most walk with a lofty [noble] chin. Of complexion, black, but by design, as the gypsies in England: They grease themselves with bear's fat clarified, and using no defense against sun or weather, their skins must needs be swarthy [dark].

Their eye is little and black, not unlike a straight-looked Jew; the thick lip and flat nose, so frequent with the East Indians and Blacks, are not common to them; for I have seen as comely European-like faces among them of both, as on your side of the sea; and truly an Italian complexion hath not much more of the white, and the noses of several of them have as much of the Roman.

XII. Their language is lofty, yet narrow, but like the Hebrew; in signification full, like short-hand in writing; one word serveth in the place of three, and the rest are supplied by the understanding of the hearer.... I have made it my business to understand it, that I might not want an interpreter on any occasion. And I must say, that I know not a language spoken in Europe that hath words of more sweetness and greatness, in accent and emphasis, than theirs....

VXI. Their diet is maize, or Indian corn, diverse ways prepared: sometimes roasted in the ashes, sometimes beaten and boiled with water, which they call Homine. They also make cakes, not unpleasant to eat. They likewise eat several sorts of beans and peas that are good nourishment....

XIX ...in liberality [generosity] they excell; nothing is too good for their friend. Give them a fine gun, coat, or any other thing, it may pass twenty hands, before it sticks. Light of heart, strong affections, but soon spent; the most merry creatures that live, feast and dance perpetually....

Some kings have sold, others presented me with several parcels of land; the pay or presents I made them were not hoarded by the particular owners, but the neighboring kings and their clans being present when the goods were brought out, the parties chiefly concerned consulted, what and to whom they should be give them? To every king then, . . . is a proportion sent. . . . Then that king subdivideth it in like manner among his dependents, they hardly leaving themselves an equal share with one of their subjects; and be it on such occasions, at festivals, or at their common meals, the kings distribute, and to themselves last . . . [the kings divide their lands before keeping any for themselves].

Since the European came into these parts, they [Native Americans] are grown [have become] great lovers of strong liquors, rum especially, and for it exchange the richest of their skins and furs. If they are heated [drunk] with liquors, they are restless till they have enough to sleep. That is their cry, Some more, and I will go to sleep; but when drunk, one of the most wretchedest spectacles in the world.

XX.   In sickness, [they are] impatient to be cured, and for it give anything, especially for their children, to whom they are extremely natural [i.e., to whom they show natural affection]. They drink at those times a Teran or decoction [extract] of some roots in spring water; and if they eat any flesh, it must be of the female of any creature. If they die, they bury them with their apparel, be they men or women, and the nearest kin fling in something precious with them, as a token of their love. Their mourning is blacking of their face, which they continue for a year. . . .

XXII.   Their government is by kings, which they call Sachema, and those by succession, but always of the mother's side. For instance, the children of him that is now king, will not succeed, but his brother by the mother, or the children of his sister, whose sons (and after them the children of her daughters) will reign; for no woman inherits. The reason they render [agree on] for this way of descent is that their issue may not be spurious [of illegitimate birth]. . . .

XIII.   Every king hath his council, and that consists of all the old and wise men of his nation. . . . 'Tis admirable to consider, how powerful the kings are, and yet how they move by the breath of their people. I have had occasion to be in council with them upon treaties for land, and to adjust the terms of trade.

Their order is thus: The king sits in the middle of an half moon [half circle], and hath his council, the old and wise on each hand; behind them, or at a little distance, sit the younger fry [youngsters], in the same figure. Having consulted and resolved their business, the king ordered one of them to speak to me; he stood up, came to me, and in the name of his king saluted me, then took me by the hand, and told me that he was ordered by his king to speak to me, and that now it was not he, but the king that spoke, because what he should say was the king's mind. He first prayed me to excuse them that they had not complied with me the last time; he feared, there might be some fault in the interpreter, being neither Indian nor English. Besides, it was the Indian custom to deliberate, and take up much time in council, before they resolve; and that if the young people or owners of the land had been as ready as he, I had not met with so much delay.

Having thus introduced the matter, he fell to the bounds of the land they had agreed to dispose of, and the price (which [land] now is little and dear, that which would have bought twenty miles, not buying now two). During this time that this person spoke, not a man of them was observed to whisper or smile; the old, grave, the young, reverent in their deportment [conduct]; they do speak little, but fervently, and with elegancy. I have never seen more natural sagacity [keenness], . . .

When the purchase was agreed, great promises passed between us of kindness and good neighborhood, and that the Indians and English must live in love, as long as the sun gave light. Which done, another made a speech to the Indians, in the name of all the Sachamakers or kings, first to tell them what was done; next, to charge and command them, to love the Christians, and particularly to live in peace with me, and the people under my government; that many governors had been in the river, but that no governor had come himself to live and stay here before; and having now such a one that had treated them well, they should never do him or his any wrong. At every sentence of which they shouted, and said Amen, in their way. . . .

XXV.   We have agreed, that in all differences between us, six of each side shall end the matter. Don't abuse them, but let them have justice, and you will win them. The worst is that they are the worse for the Christians, who have propagated [spread] their vices, and yielded them tradition for ill, and not for good things. . . .

XXVI.   For their original [origins], I am ready to believe them of the Jewish race, I mean, of the stock of the Ten [lost] Tribes. . . .

XXVII.   The first planters in these parts were Dutch, and soon after them the Swedes and Finns. The Dutch applied themselves to traffic [trade], the Swedes and Finns to husbandry [agriculture]. There were some disputes between them [for] some years, the Dutch looking upon them as intruders upon their purchase and possession, which was finally ended in the surrender made by . . . the Swedes' governor, to Peter Stuyvesont, governor for the States of Holland, Anno [in the year] 1655.

XXVIII. The Dutch inhabit mostly those parts of the province that lie upon or near to the bay, and the Swedes the freshes [newest] of the river Delaware. There is no need of giving any description of them, who are better known there than here; but they are a

To ensure peaceful relations with the Indians, William Penn drafted a treaty with the village chiefs.

plain, strong, industrious people, yet have made no great progress in culture or propagation of fruit trees, as if they desired rather to have enough, than plenty or traffic. But I presume the Indians made them the more careless, by furnishing them with the means of profit, to wit, skins and furs, for rum and such strong liquors.

They kindly received me, as well as the English, who were few, before the people concerned with me came among them. I must commend their respect to authority, and kind behavior to the English. . . .

XXXI.   Our people are mostly settled upon the upper rivers, which are pleasant and sweet, and generally bounded with good land. The planted part of the province and territories is cast into six counties: Philadelphia, Buckingham, Chester, New Castle, Kent, and Sussex, maintaining about four thousand souls. The General Assemblies have been held, and with such concord [agreement, harmony] and dispatch that they sat but three weeks, and at least seventy laws were passed without one dissent in any material thing. But of this more hereafter, being yet raw and new in our gear [adjustment].

However, I cannot forget their singular respect to me in this infancy of things, who by their own private expenses so early considered mine for the public, as to present me with an impost [tax] upon certain goods imported and exported; which after my acknowledgments of their affection, I did as freely remit to the province and traders to it. And for the well government of the said counties, courts of justice are established in every county, with proper officers, as justices, sheriffs, clerks, constables, etc., which courts are held every two months. But to prevent lawsuits, there are three peace-makers chosen by every county court, in the nature of common arbitrators, to hear and end differences betwixt [between] man and man; and spring and fall there is an orphan's court in each county, to inspect and regulate the affairs of orphans and widows.

XXXII. Philadelphia, the expectation of those that are concerned in this province, is at last laid out to the great content of those here. . . . It is advanced within less than a year to about four score [eighty] houses and cottages, such as they are, where merchants and handicrafts are following their vocations [professions] as fast as they can, while the countrymen are close at their farms. . . .

T. J. Stiles, ed., *In Their Own Words: The Colonizers.* New York: Berkeley Publishing, 1998, pp. 305–309.

German Settlers in Pennsylvania

In 1683, German Mennonites founded the settlement of Germantown in Pennsylvania. Here, Francis D. Pastorius, an agent for the land company that sponsored the venture, describes the experience.

The governor, William Penn, laid out the city of Philadelphia between the two rivers Delaware and Schuylkill, naming it with the pious wish . . . that its inhabitants might dwell together in brotherly love and unity. . . .

The inhabitants may be divided into three classes: (1) the aborigines, or, as they are called, the savages; (2) those Christians who have been in the country for years and are called old settlers; (3) the newly arrived colonists of the different companies. . . .

The aborigines of this country had their own chiefs and kings. We Christians acknowledge as our . . . chief magistrate the . . . Hon. William Penn, to whom this region was granted . . . by His Majesty of England, Charles II, with the express command that all the previous and future colonists should be subject to Penn's laws and jurisdiction.

This wise and truly pious . . . governor did not, however, take possession of the province thus granted without having first . . . duly purchased from, the natives . . . the various regions of Pennsylvania. . . . I therefore have purchased from him some 30,000 acres for my German colony.

William Penn is . . . of the sects of Friends, or Quakers . . . , but he has granted to everyone free . . . exercise of their opinions and . . . complete liberty of conscience. . . .

In my newly laid out Germantown there are already sixty-four families in a very prosperous condition. . . . We are employing the wild inhabitants . . . and we ourselves are gradually learning their language, so to instruct them in the religion of Christ.

Albert Bushnell Hart, ed., *American History Told by Contemporaries.* Vol. I. *Era of Colonization, 1492–1689.* 1896. Reprint, New York: Macmillan, 1925.

An Account of East New Jersey

In an attempt to attract people to the East New Jersey colony, three of the area's settlers wrote the following account.

For the encouragement of all our countrymen who may be inclinable to come into this Countrey [we give] you this brief and true account of it. . . . A great deal of [the land] is naturally clear of wood, And what is not so, is easily cleared, the trees being but small and a good distance from one another, so that the Land yet untaken up [unsettled] . . . is easier to clear than that which is taken up, the Towns that are already seated [established], being seated in the woodiest places.

The Merchants in *New York*, both *Dutch* and *English*, have many of them taken up land among us, and settled Plantations in this Countrey, and severall from that Collony are desiring to come and take up land among us, though they might have land in their own Collony without paying Quitt rents [land rental fees]. . . .

There be People of several sorts of Religion, but few very Zealous. The People being mostly *New England* men, doe mostly incline to their way, and in every Town there is a meeting house where they worship publickly every Week. . . .

There are few *Indian Natives* in this Countrey. Their strength is inconsiderably, they live in the Woods, and have small towns in some places far up in the Countrey. . . . They have *Kings* among themselves to govern them. For *Religion*, they have none at all.

Albert Bushnell Hart, ed., *American History Told by Contemporaries.* Vol. I. *Era of Colonization, 1492–1689.* 1896. Reprint, New York: Macmillan, 1925.

"What Dangerous and Bad Consequences"

The question of whether or not to legalize slavery was a divisive issue during the early history of Georgia, a colony in which slavery was prohibited. In 1738, the citizens of Savannah, Georgia, signed a petition asking that the antislavery laws be repealed. In response, citizens of the small town of Darien sent a counter petition, excerpted here, requesting that slavery remain illegal in the colony.

We are informed, that our Neighbors of Savannah have petitioned your Excellency [Georgia's governor-general James Oglethorpe] for the Liberty of having Slaves. We hope and earnestly entreat, that before such Proposals are hearkened [heard, implemented] unto, your Excellency will consider our Situation, and of what dangerous and bad Consequence such liberty would be of to us, for many Reasons;

I. The Nearness of the Spaniard [in nearby Florida], who have proclaimed Freedom to all Slaves who run away from their Masters, makes it impossible for us to keep them [slaves] without more Labour in guarding them, that what we would be at to do their Work.

II. We are laborious, and know that a White Man may be by the Year more usefully employed than a Negro.

III. We are not rich, and becomeing Debtors for Slaves, in case of their running away or dying, would inevitably ruin the poor Master, and he become a great Slave to the Negro Merchant, than the Slave he bought could be to him.

IV. It would oblige us to keep a Guard-duty at least as severe as when we expected a daily Invasion; and if that was the Case, how miserable would it be to us, and our Wives and Families, to have an Enemy without, and more dangerous ones in our Bosom!

V. It's shocking to human Nature, that any Race of Mankind, and their Posterity, should be sentenced to perpetual Slavery; nor in Justice can we think otherwise of it, than they are thrown amongst us to be our Scourge one Day or another for our Sins; and as Freedom to them must be as dear as to us, what a Scene of Horror must it bring about! And the longer it is unexecuted, the bloody Scene must be the greater. We therefore, for our own sakes, our Wives and Children, and our Posterity, beg your Consideration, and intreat, that instead of introducing Slaves, you'll put us in the way to get us some of our Countrymen, who with their Labour in time of Peace, and our Vigilance, if we are invaded, with the Help of those, will render it a difficult thing to hurt us, or that Part of the Province we possess. We will for ever pray for your Excellency, and are, with all Submission,

Your Excellency's most obliged
humble Servants

Colonial Records of the State of Georgia. Atlanta: 1905.

Chapter Three

Life in the Colonies

When the first English settlers arrived in the New World, they brought with them their own traditions, family structures, and ways of life. They integrated these ideals into their newly formed societies but soon discovered that many of the old ways were not designed for life in America. Class structures, farming methods, building techniques—all had to be altered to suit a climate and terrain that was much different from what the early settlers had known in Europe.

Traditional social status, for example, became obsolete. Most of the people who settled in the American colonies were neither very wealthy nor very poor. Instead, they were craftsmen or businessmen who traveled across the Atlantic in search of a place to establish a profitable trade. Thus, the New World became a land of opportunity, one in which common men—the sons of laborers or farmers—could rise in status and class. Benjamin Franklin was one who took advantage of this. The son of a candle maker in Boston, Massachusetts, Franklin became a publisher, scientist, and gentleman in Philadelphia, Pennsylvania; he also helped draft the Declaration of Independence.

Such climbs in social status, however, were reserved for free, white men. The lives of indentured servants (people whose masters brought them to America in exchange for a certain length of servitude), slaves, and women remained second-class. Slaves, for instance, were bought and sold on the auction block, and women were expected to subjugate themselves to their husbands' beliefs. These people had little or no recourse to escape their lifestyle. In fact, they could be subjected to physical punishment if they tried to make a change.

Children's lives were not much better. Strict Puritanical ideals became the norm in households and schools throughout the colonies. Children didn't play; they worked alongside their parents. They studied and prepared themselves for lives of hard labor and family responsibilities.

Life in the colonies was difficult. Settlers were charged with the task of building a nation from a wild landscape. They did it, though, because they recognized the possibilities—primarily the chance to raise one's societal and financial position—that came with such an endeavor.

Housing in Virginia in 1687

By 1687, Virginia had advanced beyond its crude beginnings at Jamestown. A Frenchman exiled to the colony because of his religious beliefs wrote this description of upper-class housing there.

Some people in this country are comfortably housed; the farmers' houses are built entirely of wood, the roofs being made of small boards of chestnut, as are also the walls. Those who have some means, cover them inside with a coating of mortar in which they use oyster-shells for lime; it is as white as snow, so that although they look ugly from the outside, where only the wood can be seen, they are very pleasant inside, with convenient windows and openings. They have started making bricks in quantities, and I have seen several houses where the walls were entirely made of them. Whatever their rank, and I know not why, they build only two rooms with some closets on the ground floor, and two rooms in the attic above; but they build several like this, according to their means. They build also a separate kitchen, a separate house for the Christian slaves, one for the negro slaves, and several to dry the tobacco, so that when you come to the home of a person of some means, you think you are entering a fairly large village. There are no stables because they never lock up their cattle. Indeed few of the houses have a lock, for nothing is ever stolen.

Warren M. Billings, ed., *The Old Dominion in the Seventeenth Century: A Documentary History of Virginia, 1606–1689*. Chapel Hill: University of North Carolina Press, 1975.

In His Own Words

Colonist Benjamin Franklin became one of America's best known scientists, writers, and politicians. In this excerpt from his autobiography, Franklin describes his first seventeen years, including his early years as a printer's apprentice and his trip from Boston to Philadelphia. His account reveals much about everyday life in colonial America.

Between the ages of twelve and twenty-one, Benjamin Franklin worked as a printer's apprentice for his brother James.

Josiah, my father, married young, and carried his wife with three children unto New England, about 1682.... By the same wife he had four children more born there, and by a second wife ten more, in all 17, of which I remember 13 sitting at one time at his table, who all grew up to be men and women, and married. I was the youngest son [born in 1706], and the younger child but two, and was born in Boston, N. England. My mother, the second wife, was Abiah Folger, a daughter of Peter Folger, one of the first settlers of new England....

My elder brothers were all put [sent as] apprentices to different trades. I was put to the grammar school at eight years of age, my father intending to devote me as the tithe [a voluntary contribution to support the church] of his sons to the service of the Church [of England]. My early readiness in learning to read (which must have been very early, as I do not remember when I could not read) and the opinion of all his friends that I should certainly make a good scholar, encouraged him in this purpose of his. My uncle Benjamin too approved of it, and proposed to give me all his shorthand volumes of sermons, I suppose as a stock to set up with, if I would learn his character [shorthand].

I continued however at the grammar school not quite one year, tho' in that time I had risen gradually from the middle of the class of that year to be the head of it, and farther was removed into the next class above it, in order to go with that into the third at the end of the year. But my father in the meantime, from a view of the expense of a college education which, having so large a family, he could not well afford, and the mean living many so educated men were afterwards able to obtain, reasons that he gave to his friends in my hearing, altered his first intention, took me from the grammar school, and sent me to a school for writing and arithmetic kept by a then famous man, Mr. Geo. [George] Brownell.... Under him I acquired fair writing pretty soon, but I failed in the arithmetic, and made no progress in it.

At ten years old, I was taken home to assist my father in his business which was that of a tallow chandler [a person who makes tallow, the chief ingredient in soaps, candles, and lubricants] and soap boiler. A business he was not bred to, but had assumed on his arrival in New England and on finding his dying trade would not maintain his family, being in little request. Accordingly I was employed in cutting wick for the candles, filling the dipping mold, and the molds for the cast candles, attending the shop, going of errands, etc.

I disliked the trade and had a strong inclination for the sea; but my father declared against it. However, living near the water, I was much in and about it, learned early to swim well, and to manage boats, and when in a boat or canoe with other boys I was commonly allowed to govern, especially in any case of difficulty; and upon other occasions I was generally a leader among the boys, and sometimes led them into scrapes [fights]. . . .

To return. I continued thus employed in my father's business for two years, that is till I was 12 years old; and my brother John, who was bred to that business, having left my father, married and set up for himself at Rhode Island. There was all appearance that I was destined to supply his place and be a tallow chandler. But my dislike to the trade continuing, my father was under apprehensions [suspected] that if he did not find one for me more agreeable, I should break away and get to sea, as his son Josiah had done to his great vexation [trouble, distress]. He therefore sometimes took me to walk with him, and see joiners [a person who builds things by joining pieces of wood], bricklayers, turners [a person who constructs things by using a rotating machine], braziers [a person who works with brass], etc., at their work, that he might observe my inclination, and endeavor to fix it on some trade or other on land. . . .

From a child I was fond of reading, and all the little money that came into my hands was ever laid out in books. . . . This bookish inclination at length determined my father to make me a printer, tho' he had already one son (James) of that profession.

In 1717 my brother James returned from England with a press and letters to set up his business in Boston. I liked it much better than that of my father, but still had a hankering for the sea. To prevent . . . such an inclination, my father was impatient to have me bound to my brother. I stood out some time, but at last was persuaded and signed the indentures [a contract binding one person to work for another for a given period of time], when I was yet but 12 years old. I was to serve as an apprentice till I was 21 years of age, only I was to be allowed journeyman's [a worksman who has completed his apprenticeship] wages during the last year.

In a little time I made great proficiency in the business, and became a useful hand to my brother. I now had access to better books. An acquaintance with the apprentices of booksellers enabled me sometimes to borrow a small one, which I was careful to return soon and clean. Often I sat up on my room reading the greatest part of the night, when the book was borrowed in the evening and to be returned early in the morning, lest it should be missed or wanted. . . .

My brother had in 1720 or 21 begun to print a newspaper. It was the second that appeared in America, and was called *The New England Courant.* The only one before it was *The Boston News Letter.* I remember his being dissuaded by some of his friends from the undertaking, as not likely to succeed, one newspaper being in their judgment enough for America. . . . He went on, however, with the undertaking, and after having worked in composing the types and printing off the sheets I was employed to carry the papers thro' the streets to meet customers.

He had some ingenious [clever, resourceful] men among his friends who amused themselves by writing little pieces for this paper, which gained it credit, and made it more in demand; and these gentlemen often visited us. Hearing their conversations, and their accounts of the approbation [praise] their papers were received with, I was excited to try my hand among them. But being still a boy, and suspecting that my brother would object to printing anything of mine in his paper if he knew it to be mine, I contrived [planned] to disguise my hand [handwriting], and writing an anonymous paper I put it in at night under the door of the printing house.

It was found in the morning and communicated to his writing friends when they called in as usual. They read it, commented on it in my hearing, and I had the exquisite pleasure of finding it met with their approbation, and that in their different guesses at the author, none were named but men of some character among us for learning and ingenuity, I suppose now that I was rather lucky in my judges, and that perhaps they were not really so very good ones as I esteemed them.

Encouraged however by this, I wrote and conveyed in the same way to the press several more papers, which were equally approved, and I kept my secret till my small fund of sense for such performances was pretty well exhausted, and then I discovered [revealed] it; when I began to be considered a little more by my brother's acquaintances, and in a manner that did not quite please him, as he thought, probably with reason, that it tended to make me too vain.

And perhaps this might be one occasion of the differences that we frequently had about this time. Tho' a brother, he considered himself as my master, and me as his apprentice; and accordingly expected the same services from me as he would from another; while I thought he demeaned me too much in some he required of me, who from a brother expected more indulgence. Our disputes were often brought before our father, and I fancy I was either generally in the right, or else a better pleader, because the judgment was generally in my favor. But my brother was passionate and had often beaten me, which I took extremely amiss; and thinking my apprenticeship very tedious, I was constantly wishing for some opportunity of shortening it, which at length offered in a manner unexpected.

One of the pieces in our newspaper, on some political point which I have now forgotten, gave offense to the Assembly. He [Franklin's brother] was taken up, censured [criticized, blamed], and imprisoned for a month ... , I suppose because he would not discover his author. I too was taken up and examined before the Council; but tho' I did not give them any satisfaction, they contented themselves with admonishing me, and dismissed me; considering me perhaps as an apprentice, who was bound to keep his master's secrets.

During my brother's confinement, which I resented a good deal, notwithstanding our private differences, I had the management of the paper, and I made bold to give our rulers some rubs with it, which my brother took very kindly, while others began to consider me in an unfavorable light, as a young genius that had a turn for libelling [to publish negative statements about someone without just cause] and satire [a literary work that holds up human faults to ridicule or scorn]. My brother's discharge was accompanied with an order of the House [legislature] (a very odd one) that James Franklin should no longer print the paper called the *New England Courant*.

There was a consideration held in our printing house among his friends what he should do in this case. Some proposed to evade [avoid] the order by changing the name of the paper, but my brother, seeing the inconveniences in that, it was finally concluded on as a better way, to let it be printed for the future under the name of *Benjamin Franklin*. And to avoid the censure of the Assembly that might fall on him, as still printing it by his apprentice, the contrivance was that my old indenture should be returned to me with a full discharge on the back of it, to be shown on occasion; but to secure to him the benefit of my service I was to sign new indentures for the remainder of the term, which were to be kept private.

A very flimsy scheme it was, but however, it was immediately executed, and the paper went on accordingly under my name for several months. At length a fresh difference arising between my brother and me, I took upon me to assert my freedom, presuming that he would not venture to produce the new indentures. It was not fair in me to take this advantage, and this I therefore reckon one of the first errata [errors] of my life. But the unfairness of it weighed little with me. . . .

When he found I would leave him, he took care to prevent my getting employment in any other printing house of the town, by going round and speaking to every master, who accordingly refused to give me work. I then thought of going to New York as the nearest place where there was a printer; and I was rather inclined to leave Boston, when I reflected that I had already made myself a little obnoxious to the governing party; and from the arbitrary proceedings of the Assembly in my brother's case it was likely I might if I stayed soon bring myself into scrapes; and farther that my indiscreet disputations [unwise arguments] about religion begun to make me pointed at with horror by good people, as an infidel [one who is not a Christian] or atheist.

I determined on the point; but my father now siding with my brother, I was sensible that if I attempted to go openly, men would be used to prevent me. My friend Collins therefore undertook to manage a little for me. He agreed with the captain of a New York sloop [a type of boat] for my passage, under the notion of my being a young acquaintance of his that had got a naughty girl with child. . . . So I sold some of my books to raise a little money, was taken on board privately, and as we had a fair wind in three days I found myself in New York, near 300 miles from home, a boy of but 17, without the least recommendation to or knowledge of any person in the place, and with very little money in my pocket. . . .

I offered by service to the printer of the place, old Mr. William Bradford (who had been the first printer in Pennsylvania, but removed from thence upon the quarrel of [Governor] George Keith). He could give me no employment, having little to do, and help enough already. But, says he, my son at Philadelphia has lately lost his principal hand, Aquila Rose, by death. If you go thither I believe he may employ you. . . .

[I] arrived there [in Philadelphia] about 8 or 9 o'clock, in the Sunday morning, and landed at the Market Street wharf. . . . I was in my working dress, my best clothes being to come round by sea. I was dirty from my journey; my pockets were stuffed out with shirts and stockings; I knew no soul, nor where to look for lodging. I was fatigued with travelling, rowing, and want of rest. I was very hungry, and my whole stock of cash consisted of a Dutch dollar and about a shilling [a former monetary unit] in copper. The latter I gave the people of the boat for my passage, who at first refused it on account of my rowing; but I insisted in their taking it, a man being sometimes more generous when he has but a little money than when he has plenty, perhaps thro' fear of being thought to have but little.

Then I walked up the street, gazing about, till . . . I met a boy with bread. I had made many a meal on bread, and inquiring where he got it, I went immediately to the baker's he directed me to in Second Street; and asked for biscuit, intending such as we had in Boston, but they it seems were not made in Philadelphia. Then I asked for a three-penny loaf, and was told they had none such, so not considering or knowing the difference of money and the greater cheapness nor the names of his bread, I bade him give me three penny worth of any sort. He gave me accordingly three great puffy rolls. I was surprised at the quantity, but took it, and having no room in my pockets, walked off, with a roll under each arm, and eating the other. . . .

Thus refreshed I walked again up the street, which by this time had many clean dressed people in it who were all walking the same way. I joined them, and thereby was led into the great Meeting

House of the Quakers. . . . I sat down among them, and after looking round a while and hearing nothing said, being very drowsy thro' labor and want of rest the preceding night, I fell asleep, and continued to till the meeting broke up, when one was kind enough to rouse me. This was therefore the first house I was in or slept in, in Philadelphia. . . .

I began now to have some acquaintance among the young people of the town, that were lovers of reading, with whom I spent my evenings very pleasantly. And gaining money by my industry and frugality [thriftiness], I lived very agreeably, forgetting Boston as much as I could. . . .

T. J. Stiles, ed., *In Their Own Words: The Colonizers.* New York: Berkeley Publishing, 1998.

Impressions of New Jersey and New York

As Per (Peter) Kalm, a Swede, traveled through the northern colonies during the mid-eighteenth century, he recorded his impressions of the land he saw and the people he met. The accounts excerpted below describe his impressions of New Jersey and New York.

Trenton [New Jersey] is a long narrow town, situated at some distance from the Delaware River, on a sandy plain; it belongs to New Jersey, and they reckon it thirty miles from Philadelphia. . . . [F]rom Trenton to New Brunswick [New Jersey], the travellers go in wagons which set out every day for that place. Several of the inhabitants however subsist [live] on the transportation of all sorts of goods, which are sent every day in great quantities, either from Philadelphia to New York, or from there to the former place. Between Philadelphia and Trenton all goods are transported by water, but between Trenton and New Brunswick they are carried by land, and both these means of transportation belong to people of this town. . . .

We continued our journey in the morning; the country through which we passed was for the greatest part level, though sometimes there were some long hills; some parts were covered with trees, but by far the greater part of the country was without woods; on the other hand I never saw any place in America, the city excepted, so well peopled. An old man, who lived in the neighborhood and accompanied us a short distance, assured me however that he could well remember the time when between Trenton and New Brunswick there were not above three farms, and he reckoned it was about fifty and some odd years ago. During the greater part of the day we saw very extensive cultivated fields on both sides of the road, and we observed that the country generally had a noticeable declivity [sloping down] towards the south. Near almost every farm was a spacious orchard full of peaches and apple trees, and in some of them the fruit had fallen from the trees in such quantities as to cover nearly the whole surface of the ground. Part of it they left to rot, since they could not take care of it all or consume it. Wherever we passed by we were welcome to go into the fine orchards and gather our hats and pockets full of the choicest fruit, without the owner so much as looking at us. Cherry trees were planted near the farms, on the roads, etc.

The *barns* had a peculiar kind of construction in this locality, of which I shall give a concise description. The main building was very large almost the size of a small church; the roof was high, covered with wooden shingles, sloping on both sides, but not steep. The walls which supported it were not much higher than a full grown man; but on the other hand the breadth [width] of the building was all the greater. In the middle was the threshing floor and above it, or in the loft or garret, they put the unthreshed grain, the straw, or anything else, according to the season. On one side were stables for the horses, and on the other for the cows. The young stock had also their particular stables or stalls, and in both ends of the building were large doors, so that one could drive in with a cart and horses through one of them, and go out at the other. Here under one roof therefore were the thrashing floor, the barn, the stables, the hayloft, the coach house, etc. This kind of building is used chiefly by the Dutch and Germans, for it is to be observed that the country between Trenton and New York is not inhabited by many Englishmen, but mostly by Germans or Dutch, the latter of which are especially numerous.

Indians

Before I proceed I must mention one thing about the Indians or old Americans, for this account may find readers, who, like many people of my acquaintance, have the opinion that North America is almost wholly inhabited by savage or heathen nations; and they may be astonished that I do not mention them more frequently in my account. Others may perhaps imagine that when I state in my journal that the country is widely cultivated, that in several places houses of stone or wood are built, round which are grain fields, gardens and orchards, that I am speaking of the property of the Indians. To undeceive them I shall here give the following explanation. The country, especially that along the coasts in the English colonies, is inhabited by Europeans, who in some places are already so numerous that few parts of Europe are more populous [densely settled]. The Indians have sold the land to the Europeans, and have retired further inland. In most parts you may travel twenty Swedish miles, or about a hundred and twenty English miles, from the coast, before you reach the first habitation of the Indians. And it is very possible for a person to have been at Philadelphia and other towns on the seashore for half a year without so much as seeing an Indian....

About noon we arrived at New Brunswick, (situated about thirty miles from Trenton and sixty from Philadelphia), a pretty little town in the province of New Jersey, in a valley on the west side of the river Raritan. On account of its low location, it cannot be seen (coming from Pennsylvania) before you get to the top of the hill, which is quite close to it. The town extends north and south along the river. The German inhabitants have two churches, one of stone and the other of wood. The English church is likewise of the latter material, but the Presbyterians are building one of stone. The Town Hall makes a good appearance. Some of the other houses are built of brick, but most of them are made either wholly of wood, or of brick and wood. The wooden buildings are not made of strong timber, but merely of boards or planks, which are within joined by laths [narrow strips of wood]. Houses built of both wood and brick have only the wall towards the street made of the latter, all the other sides being boards. This peculiar kind of ostentation [excessive display] would easily lead a traveller who passes through the

Early colonial houses in New Brunswick were built mostly of wood or brick and wood.

town in haste to believe that most of the houses are built of brick. The houses are covered with shingles. Before each door is a veranda to which you ascend by steps from the street; it resembles a small balcony, and has benches on both sides on which the people sit in the evening to enjoy the fresh air and to watch the passers-by. The town has only one street lengthways, and at its northern extremity [farthest point] there is a cross street: both of these are of a considerable length.

The river Raritan passes close by the town, and is deep enough for large sailing vessels. Its breadth near the town is about the distance of a common gun shot. The tide comes up several miles beyond the town, which contributes not a little to the ease and convenience of securing vessels which dock along the bridge. The river has generally very high and steep banks on both sides, but near the town there are no such banks, because it is situated in a low valley. One of the streets is almost entirely inhabited by Dutchmen who came hither from Albany [New York], and for that reason it is called Albany Street.

These Dutch people keep company only with themselves, and seldom or never go amongst the other inhabitants, living as it were quite separate from them. . . .

The Jews

Besides the different sects of Christians, many Jews have settled in New York, who possess great privileges. They have a synagogue, own their dwelling-houses, possess large country-seats [houses or estates in the country] and are allowed to keep shops in town. They have likewise several ships, which they load and send out with their own goods. In fine, they enjoy all the privileges common to the other inhabitants of this town and province. . . .

During my residence in New York, both at this time and for the next two years, I was frequently in company with Jews. I was informed among other things that these people never boiled any meat for themselves on Saturday, but that they always did it the day before, and that in winter they kept a fire during the whole Saturday. They commonly eat no pork; yet I have been told by several trustworthy men that many of them (especially the young Jews) when travelling, "did not hesitate the least about eating this or any other meat that was" put before them, even though they were in company with Christians. I was in their synagogue last evening for the first time, and today at noon I visited it again, and each time I was put in a special seat which was set apart for strangers or Christians. A young rabbi read the devine service, which was partly in Hebrew and partly in the Rabinical dialect. Both men and women were dressed entirely in the English fashion; the former had their hats on, and did not once take them off during the service. The galleries [balconies], I observed, were reserved for the ladies, while the men sat below. During prayers the men spread a white cloth over their heads, which perhaps is to represent sackcloth [a coarse cloth]. But I observed that the wealthier sort of people had a much richer cloth than the poorer ones. Many of the men had Hebrew books, in which they sang and read alternately. The rabbi stood in the middle of the synagogue and read with his face turned towards the east; he spoke however so fast as to make it almost impossible for any one to understand what he said. . . .

The First Colonists

The first *colonists* in New York were Dutchmen. When the town and its territories were taken by the English and left to them by the next peace in exchange for Surinam [Suriname, a country in South America], the old inhabitants were allowed either to remain at New York, and enjoy all the privileges and immunities which they were possessed of before, or to leave the place with all their goods. Most of them chose the former; and therefore the inhabitants both of the town and of the province belonging to it are still for the greatest part Dutch, who still, and especially the old people, speak their mother tongue.

They were beginning however by degrees to change their manners and opinions, chiefly indeed in the town and in its neighborhood; for most of the young people now speak principally English, go only to the English church, and would even take it amiss if they were called Dutchmen and not Englishmen. . . .

The Dutch Settlers

But the lack of people in this province may likewise be accounted for in a different manner. As the Dutch, who first cultivated this section, obtained the liberty of staying here by the treaty with England, and of enjoying all their privileges and advantages without the least limitation, each of them took a very large piece of ground for himself, and many of the more powerful heads of families made themselves the possessors and masters of a country of as great territory as would be sufficient to form one of our moderately-sized, and even one of our large, parishes. Most of them being very rich, their envy of the English led them not to sell them any land, but at an excessive rate, a practice which is still punctually observed among their descendants. The English therefore, as well as people of other nations, have but little encouragement to settle here. On the other hand, they have sufficient opportunity in the other provinces to purchase land at a more moderated price, and with more security to themselves. It is not to be wondered then, that so many parts of New York are still uncultivated, and that it has entirely the appearance of a frontier-land. This instance may teach us how much a small mistake in a government can hamper the settling of a country. . . .

Trade

Albany [in upstate New York] carries on a considerable commerce with New York [City], chiefly in furs, boards, wheat, flour, peas, several kinds of timber, etc. There is not a place in all the British colonies, the Hudson's Bay settlements excepted, where such quantities of furs and skins are bought of the Indians as at Albany. Most of the merchants in this town send a clerk or agent to Oswego, an English trading town on Lake Ontario, to which the Indians come with their furs. I intend to give a more minute account of this place in my Journal for the year 1750. The merchants from Albany spend the whole summer at Oswego, and trade with many tribes of Indians who come with their goods. Many people have assured me that the Indians are frequently cheated in disposing of their goods, especially when they are drunk, and that sometimes they do not get one half or even one tenth of the value of their goods. I have been a witness to several transactions of this kind. The merchants of Albany glory in these tricks, and are highly pleased when they have given a poor Indian, a greater portion of brandy than he can stand, and when they can, after that, get all his goods for mere trifles [something of little value]. The Indians often find when they are sober again, that they have for once drunk as much as they are able of a liquor which they value beyond anything else in the whole world, and they are quite insensible to their loss if they again get a draught [drink] of this nectar. Besides this trade at Oswego, a number of Indians come to Albany from several places especially from Canada; but from this latter place, they hardly bring anything but beaver skins. . . .

The Dutch in Albany

The inhabitants of Albany and its environs [surroundings] are almost all Dutchmen. They speak Dutch, have Dutch preachers, and the divine service is performed in that language. Their manners are likewise quite Dutch: their dress is however like that of the English. It is well known that the first Europeans who settled in the province of New York were Dutchmen. During the time that they were the masters of this province, they seized New Sweden of which they were jealous. However, the pleasure of possessing this conquered land and their own was but of short duration, for towards the end of 1664 Sir Robert Carr, by order of King Charles the second, went to New York then New Amsterdam, and took it. Soon after Colonel Nicolls went to Albany, which then bore the name of Fort Orange, and upon taking it, named it Albany, from the Duke of York's Scotch title. The Dutch inhabitants were allowed either to continue where they were, and under the protection of the English to enjoy all their former privileges, or to leave the country. The greater part of them chose to stay and from them the Dutchmen are descended who now live in the province of New York, and who possess the greatest and best estates in that province.

The avarice [greed], selfishness and immeasurable love of money of the inhabitants of Albany are very well known throughout all North America, by the French and even by the Dutch, in the lower part of New York province. I was here obliged to pay for everything twice, thrice and four times as much as in any part of North America which I have passed through. If I wanted their assistance, I was obliged to pay them very well for it, and when I wanted to purchase anything or be helped in some case or other, I could at once see what kind of blood ran in their veins, for they either fixed exorbitant [excessive] prices for their services or were very reluctant to assist me. Such was this people in general. However, there were some among them who equalled any in North America or anywhere else, in politeness, equity, goodness, and readiness to serve and to oblige; but their number fell far short of that of the former. If I may be allowed to declare my conjectures [conclusions], the origin of the inhabitants of Albany and its neighborhood seems to me to be as follows. While the Dutch possessed this country, and intended to people it, the government sent a pack of vagabonds of which they intended to clear their native country, and sent them along with a number of other settlers to this province. The vagabonds were sent far from the other colonists, upon the borders towards the Indians and other enemies, and a few honest families were persuaded to go with them, in order to keep them in bounds. I cannot in any other way account for the difference between the inhabitants of Albany and the other descendants of so respectable a nation as the Dutch, who are settled in the lower part of New York province. The latter are civil, obliging, just in prices, and sincere; and though they are not ceremonious [conventionally polite], yet they are well meaning and honest and their promises may be relied on. . . .

Dutch Food

The whole region about the Hudson River above Albany is inhabited by the Dutch: this is true of Saratoga as well as other places. During my stay with them I had an opportunity of observing their way of living, so far as food is concerned, and wherein they differ from other Europeans. Their breakfast here in the country was as follows: they drank tea in the customary way by putting brown sugar into the cup of tea. With the tea they ate bread and butter and radishes; they would take a bite of the bread and butter and would cut off a piece of the radish as they ate. They spread the butter upon the bread and it was each one's duty to do this for himself. They sometimes had small round cheeses (not especially fine tasting) on the table, which they cut into thin slices and spread upon the buttered bread. At noon they had a regular meal and I observed nothing unusual about it. In the evening they made a porridge of corn, poured it as customary into a dish, made a large hole in the center into which they poured fresh milk, but more often buttermilk. They ate it taking half a spoonful of porridge and half of milk. As they ordinarily took more milk than porridge, the milk in the dish was soon consumed. Then more milk was poured in. This was their supper nearly every evening. After that they would eat some meat left over from the noon-day meal, or bread and butter with cheese. If any of the porridge remained from the evening, it was boiled with buttermilk in the morning so that it became almost like a gruel. In order to make the buttermilk more tasty, they added either syrup or sugar, after it had been poured into the dish. Then they stirred it so that all of it should be equally sweet. Pudding or pie, the Englishman's perpetual dish, one seldom saw among the Dutch, neither here nor in Albany. But they were indeed fond of meat. . . .

Karen Ordahl Kupperman, ed., *Major Problems in American Colonial History.* Lexington, MA: D.C. Heath, 1993.

The Life of Elizabeth Ashbridge . . .

During the colonial period (and for many years before and after), women in America were considered intellectually, morally, and physically inferior to their husbands. As a result, women had to defer to their husbands' will or risk physical punishment and had to ask permission to do any number of things, including pursue the religion of their choice. Here, Elizabeth Ashbridge, a Quaker, tells of her struggle to maintain her faith despite being mistreated by her alcoholic husband, an Anglican who did not approve of the Quakers.

When meeting-time came, I longed to go, but dared not to ask my husband's leave. As the Friends [members of the Quaker church] were getting ready themselves, they asked him if he would accompany them, observing, that they knew whose who were to be his employers, and, if they were at meeting, would speak to them. He consented. The woman Friend then said, "And wilt thou let thy wife go too;" which request he denied; but she answered his objections so prudently [wisely] that he could not be angry, and at last consented. I went with joy, and a heavenly meeting it was. . . .

By the end of the week, we got settled in our new situation [jobs]. We took a room, in a friend's house, one mile from each school [Ashbridge and her husband were both teachers], and eight from the meeting-house. I now deemed [considered] it proper to let my husband see I was determined to join with friends. When first day came, I directed myself to him in this manner: "My dear, art thou [are you] willing to let me go to meeting?" He flew into a rage, and replied "No you sha'n't [shall not]. "Speaking firmly, I told him, "That, as a dutiful wife, I was ready to obey all his lawful commands; but, when they imposed upon my conscience, I could not obey him. I had already wronged myself, in having done it too long; and though he was near to me, and, as a wife ought, I loved him, yet God, who was nearer than all the world to me, had made me sensible that this was the way in which I ought to go. I added, that this was no small cross to my own will; but I had given up my heart, and I trusted that He who called for it would enable me, for the remainder of my life, to keep it steadily devoted to his service; and I hoped I should not, on this account, make the worse wife." I spoke, however, to no purpose,—he continued inflexible. . . .

Finding that all the means he had yet used could not alter my resolutions, he several times struck me with severe blows. I endeavoured to bear all with patience, believing that the time would come when he would see I was in the right. Once he came up to me, took out his penknife, and said, "If you offer to go to meeting to-morrow, with this knife I'll cripple you, for you shall not be a Quaker".

Giles Gunn, ed., *Early American Writing*. New York: Penguin Books, 1994.

The Pleasures of Country Life

The following poem, written by American colonial poet Ruth Belknap, describes the life of a colonial housewife.

All summer long I toil & sweat
Blister my hands, and scold & fret.
And when the summer's work is o'er,
New toils arise from Autumn's store.
Corn must be husk'd, and pork be kill'd.
The house with all confusion fill'd.
O could you see the grand display
Upon our annual butchering day,—
See me look like ten thousand sluts,
My kitchen spread with grease & guts.

Giles Gunn, ed., *Early American Writing*. New York: Penguin Books, 1994.

Children's Behavior

Children in the colonies were expected to be respectful, quiet, and polite. The following excerpts describe rules for certain social situations.

Behavior at the Table

Never sit down at the table till asked, and [only] after the blessing. Ask for nothing; tarry [wait] till it be offered thee. Speak not. Bite not thy bread but break it. Take salt only with a clean knife. Dip not the meat in the same. Hold not thy knife upright but sloping, and lay it down at right hand of plate with blade on plate. Look not earnestly at any other that is eating. When moderately satisfied leave the table. Sing not, hum not, wriggle not. Spit no where in the room but in the corner. . . .

Courtesy and Respect

Run not Hastily in the Street, nor go too Slowly. Wag not to and fro, nor use any Antick Postures either of thy Head, Hands, Feet or Body. Throw naught aught on the street, as Dirt or Stones. If thou meetest the scholars of any other School jeer not nor affront them, but show them love and respect and quietly let them pass along.

"Implicit Prompt Obedience"

A boy was early taught a profound respect for his parents, teachers, and guardians, and implicit prompt obedience. If he undertook to rebel his will was broken by persistent and adequate punishment. He was taught that it was a sin to find fault with his meals, his apparel, his tasks or his lot in life. Courtesy was enjoined as a duty. He must be silent among his superiors. If addressed by older persons he must respond with a bow. He was to bow as he entered and left the school, and to every man and woman, old or young, rich or poor, black or white, whom he met on the road. Special punishment was visited on him if he failed to show respect for the aged, the poor, the colored, or to any persons whatever whom God had visited with infirmities.

Alice Morse Earle, *Child Life in Colonial Days*. New York: Macmillan, 1899; reprinted Stockbridge, MA: Berkshire House Publishers, 1993.

"The Same Story Over Again"

The life of an aristocratic colonial child was filled with routine and monotony. Here, young Maria Carter, daughter of a Virginia plantation owner, writes her cousin about a typical day.

March 25th 1756
My Dear Cousin

You have really imposed a Task upon me which I can [by] no means perform, viz [namely] that of writing a merry & comical letter, how shou'd [I] . . . my dear that I am ever confined either at School or with my Grand-mama[.] [You?] know how the World goes on. Now . . . I will give you the history of one Day, the Repetition of which without variation carries me through the Three hundred & sixty five Days which you know compleats the year. Well then first to begin, I am awakened out of a sound Sleep with some croaking voice either Patty's, Milly's, or some other of our Domestics [house servants] with Miss Polly Miss Polly get up, tis time to rise, Mr. Price [her tutor?] is downstairs, & tho' I hear them I lie quite snug till my Grand-mamma raises her Voice, then up I get, huddle on my Cloathes & down to the Book [lessons], and then to Breakfast, then to School again & may be I have an hour to my self before Diner & then the same Story over again till twi-Light, & then a small portion of time before I go to rest, and so you must expect nothing from me but that I am

Dear Cousin
Most Affectionately Your's
Maria Carter

Manuscript. The College of William and Mary, Earl Gregg Swem Library, Manuscript and Rare Books Department.

"Fear God and Honour the King"

Religion was an important part of a colonial child's education. Here are two selections from the New England Primer, *a popular textbook of the day, which demonstrate the role religion played in colonial schools.*

The Dutiful Child's Promises (c. 1690)

I will fear GOD, and honour the KING.
I will honour my Father & Mother.
I will obey my Superiours.
I will submit to my Elders.
I will love my Friends.

I will hate no Man.
I will forgive my Enemies, and pray to God for them.
I will as much as in me lies keep all God's Holy Commandments.
I will learn my Catechism [religious instruction, usually a series
of questions and answers].
I will keep the Lord's Day Holy.
I will reverence God's sanctuary.
For our GOD is a consuming fire.

Now I Lay Me Down to Sleep (1737)
Now I lay me down to take my sleep,
I pray the Lord my soul to keep.
If I should die before I wake
I pray the Lord my soul to take.

Harry H. Warfel et al., eds., *The American Mind: Selections from the Literature of the
United States,* Volume I. New York: American Book, 1963.

"Nothing to Be Gotten Here"

*The life of an indentured servant in the colonies was a hard one. Here,
Richard Frethorne, an indentured servant, writes about his miserable
experience working on a plantation in Virginia.*

I have nothing to Comfort me, nor is there nothing to be gotten here
but sickness, and death, except that one had money to lay out in
some things for profit; But I have nothing at all, no not a shirt to my
backe, but two Rags nor no Clothes, but one poor suit, nor but one
pair of shoes, but one pair of stockings, but one Cap, but two [collar]
bands, my Cloak is stolen by one of my own fellows. . . . I am not half
a quarter so strong as I was in England, and all is for want of victuals
[food], for I do protest unto you, that I have eaten more in a day at
home than I have allowed here for a Week. You have given more than
my day's allowance to a beggar at the door.

Karen Ordahl Kupperman, ed., *Major Problems in American Colonial History.* Lexington,
MA: D. C. Heath, 1993.

Chapter Four

The Fight for Independence

The war for American independence from Great Britain officially began in 1775 when British troops marched into Lexington, Massachusetts. Unofficially, though, it started much earlier. The American colonists had, for years, become increasingly wary of the English, and by the end of the French and Indian War (a war between England and France over land in North America) in 1760, they realized that the English king had every intention of forcing them to remain a part of Great Britain.

In 1765, British Parliament passed a law, called the Stamp Act, requiring colonists to buy and place official stamps on legal documents, newspapers, pamphlets, playing cards, and other items. Because the colonists had no voice in the passage of the law, they felt the tax was unfair and refused to pay it. English soldiers and American colonists clashed violently in several cities, and, in the end, the protest was successful; the English repealed the Stamp Act.

Any glee the colonists may have felt over the victory was short-lived, however. During the next eight years, Parliament passed, and the colonists resisted, several other laws aimed at asserting British control. Then, in May 1773, Parliament passed the Tea Act, a law the colonists saw as a way for England to trick them into paying a tax on tea.

British troops march into the streets of Lexington, Massachusetts, the official beginning of the American war for independence.

The protests over this law—particularly in Boston, Massachusetts, where colonists dressed as Indians dumped forty-five tons of tea into Boston harbor—and the laws that followed set into motion a string of events that would forever alter the relationship between the colonies and Great Britain. Colonists began forming militias and stockpiling weapons. Colonial representatives met in Philadelphia, Pennsylvania, in September 1774—the first meeting of the Continental Congress— and decided to boycott all trade with Great Britain. And in April 1775, colonists and British soldiers met in the first armed conflict of the Revolutionary War.

The war would last eight years. During this time, the Continental Congress would draft the Declaration of Independence. Thousands of American men would join the Continental army, the colonies' fighting force. These soldiers would be white, black, rich, and poor.

They would be led by a general named George Washington, and even though their lives were marked by hardship, they would ultimately win their independence.

The Revolutionary Spirit

By the late 1760s, many people openly discussed the advantages of independence from Britain. This poem, written by Philip Freneau, exemplifies the revolutionary spirit that took hold of the colonies.

Too long our patient country wears her chains,
Too long our wealth all-grasping Britain drains:
Why still a handmaid to that distant land?
Why still subservient to their proud command?
Fallen on disastrous times, they scorn our plea:
'Tis our own efforts that must make us free. . . .

From the scoundrel, Lord North, who would bind us in chains.
From a dunce of a king who was born without brains.
From an island that bullies, and hectors, and swears.
I send up to heaven my wishes and prayers
That we, disunited, may freemen be still,
And Britain go on—to be damned, If she will.

Page Smith, *A New Age Now Begins.* New York: McGraw-Hill, 1976.

Parliament Questions Ben Franklin

On February 13, 1776, the British Parliament questioned colonial representative Benjamin Franklin who explained why Americans had so vigorously protested the Stamp Act.

Q. What is your name, and place of abode?
A. Franklin, of Philadelphia.
Q. Do the Americans pay any considerable taxes among themselves?
A. Certainly many, and very heavy taxes.

Q. What are the present taxes in Pennsylvania, laid by the laws of the colony?

A. There are taxes on all estates real and personal, a poll tax, a tax on all offices, professions, trades and businesses, according to their profits; an excise on all wine, rum, and other spirits; and a duty of £10 per head on all Negroes imported, with some other duties.

Q. For what purposes are those taxes laid?

A. For the support of the civil and military establishments of the country, and to discharge the heavy debt contracted in the last war [the French and Indian War]....

Q. Do you think it right that America should be protected by this country and pay no part of the expense?

A. That is not the case. The Colonies raised, cloathed and payed during the last war, near 25,000 men and spent many millions.

Q. Were you not reimbursed by Parliament?

A. We were only reimbursed what, in your opinion, we had advanced beyond our proportion, or beyond what might reasonably be expected from us; and it was a very small part of what we spent. Pennsylvania, in particular, disbursed about £500,000, and the reimbursements, in the whole, did not exceed £60,000.

Q. You have said that you pay heavy taxes in Pennsylvania. What do they amount to in the pound?

A. The tax on all estates, real and personal is eighteen pence in the pound, fully rated; and the tax on the profits of trade and professions, with other taxes, do, I suppose, make full half a crown in the pound....

Q. Do not you think the people of America would submit to pay the stamp duty if it was moderated?

A. No, never, unless compelled by force of arms....

Q. In what light did the people of America use to consider the Parliament of Great Britain?

A. They considered the Parliament as the great bulwark and security of their liberties and privileges, and always spoke of it with the utmost respect and veneration. Arbitrary ministers, they thought, might possibly, at times, attempt to oppress them; but they relied on it, that the Parliament, on application, would always give redress. They remembered with gratitude, a strong instance of this, when a bill was brought into Parliament with a clause to make royal instructions laws in the colonies, which the House of Commons would not pass, and it was thrown out.

Q. And have they not still the same respect for Parliament?

A. No, it is greatly lessened. . . .

Q. Don't you think they would submit to the Stamp Act, if it was modified, the obnoxious parts taken out, and the duty reduced to some particulars of small moment?

A. No; they will never submit to it.

Q. What is your opinion of a future tax imposed on the same principle with that of the Stamp Act? How would the Americans receive it?

A. Just as they do this. They would not pay it. . . .

Q. Don't you know that there is, in the Pennsylvania charter, an express reservation of Parliament to lay taxes there?

A. I know there is a clause in the charter by which the King [of England] grants that he will levy no taxes on the inhabitants, unless it be with the consent of the assembly or by act of Parliament.

Q. How, then, could the assembly of Pennsylvania assert that laying a tax on them by the Stamp Act was an infringement of their rights?

A. They understood it thus [this way]; by the same charter, and otherwise, they are entitled to all the privileges and liberties of Englishmen; they find in the great charters, and the petition and declaration of rights, that one of the privileges of English subjects is, that they are not to be taxed but by their common consent. They have therefore relied upon it, from the first settlement of the province, that the Parliament never would, nor could, by color of that clause in the charter, assume a right of taxing them, till it had qualified itself to exercise such right by admitting representatives from the people to be taxed, who ought to make a part of that common consent. . . .

Q. If the Stamp Act should be repealed, would it induce the assemblies of America to acknowledge the rights of Parliament to tax them, and would they erase their resolutions?

A. No, never.

Q. Are there no means of obliging them to erase those resolutions?

A. None that I know of; they will never do it, unless compelled by force of arms.

Q. Is there a power on earth that can force them to erase them?

A. No power, how great soever, can force men to change their opinions. . . .

Q. What used to be the pride of Americans?

A. To indulge in the fashions and manufactures of Great Britain.

Q. What is now their pride?

A. To wear their old clothes over again, till they can make new ones.

Richard B. Morris, ed., *The American Revolution, 1763–1783: A Bicentennial Collection.* Columbia: University of South Carolina Press, 1970.

The Loyalists Persecuted

Although many colonists supported the fight for independence, some did not. These people, called loyalists because they remained loyal to the English, sometimes became the victims of mob or random violence. This excerpt from a January 31, 1774, letter written by Boston loyalist Ann Hulton describes one such incident, the tarring and feathering of a loyalist named Malcolm.

The most shocking cruelty was exercised a few nights ago, upon a poor old man, a tidesman, one Malcolm. . . . A quarrel was picked with him, he was afterward taken and tarred and feathered. Theres no law that knows a punishment for the greatest crimes beyond what this is of cruel torture. And this instance exceeds any other before it. He was strip stark naked, one of the severest cold nights this winter, his body covered all over with tar, then with feathers, his arm dislocated in tearing off his cloaths. He was dragged in a cart with thousands attending, some beating him with clubs and knocking him out of the cart, then in again. They gave him several severe whippings, at different parts of the town. This spectacle of horror and sportive cruelty was exhibited for about five hours.

The unhappy wretch they say behaved with the greatest intrepidity [fearlessness] and fortitude all the while. Before he was taken, [he]

Outraged, Americans sometimes captured people loyal to the English and tortured them.

defended himself a long time against numbers, and afterwards when under torture they demanded of him to curse his masters, the King [of England], Governor [of Massachusetts], etc., which they could not make him do, but he still cried, "Curse all traitors!" They brought him to the gallows and put a rope about his neck, saying they would hang him. He said he wished they would, but that they could not, for God was above the Devil. The doctors say that it is impossible this poor creature can live. They say his flesh comes off his back in stakes.

It is the second time he has been tarred and feathered and this is looked upon more to intimidate the judges and others than a spite to the unhappy victim tho' they owe him a grudge for some things particularly. . . .

These few instances amongst many serve to shew the abject state of government and the licentiousness [illegality and immorality] and barbarism of the times. There's no majestrate that dare or will act to suppress the outrages. No person is secure. There are many objects pointed at, at this time, and when once marked out for vengeance, their ruin is certain.

Henry S. Commager and Richard B. Morris, eds., *The Spirit of 'Seventy-Six: The Story of the American Revolution as Told by Participants,* 2 vols. New York: Bobbs-Merrill, 1958, vol. 1.

"No Damage . . . Except to the Tea"

Many of the participants in the Boston Tea Party recorded the event as a celebrated exploit. Here, Robert Sessions recounts his activities that fateful night.

I was living in Boston at the time, in the family of a Mr. Davis, a lumber merchant, as a common laborer. On that eventful evening, when Mr. Davis came in from the town meeting, I asked him what was to be done with the tea.

"They are now throwing it overboard," he replied.

Receiving permission, I went immediately to the spot. Everything was as light as day, by the means of lamps and torches—a pin might be seen lying on the wharf. I went on board where they were at work, and took hold with my own hands.

I was not one of those appointed to destroy the tea, and who disguised themselves as Indians, but was a volunteer, the disguised men being largely men of family and position in Boston, while I was

Disguised as Indians, patriots hoisted English tea into Boston Harbor.

a young man whose home and relations were in Connecticut. The appointed and disguised party proving too small for the quick work necessary, other young men, similarly circumstanced with myself, joined them in their labors.

The chests were drawn up by a tackle—one man bringing them forward in the hold, another putting a rope around them, and others hoisting them to the deck and carrying them to the vessel's side. The chests were then opened, the tea emptied over the side, and the chests thrown overboard.

Perfect regularity prevailed during the whole transaction. Although there were many people on the wharf, entire silence prevailed—no clamor, no talking. Nothing was meddled with but the teas on board.

After having emptied the hold, the deck was swept clean, and everything put in its proper place. An officer on board was requested to come up from the cabin and see that no damage was done except to the tea.

Milton Meltzer, ed., *The American Revolutionaries: A History in Their Own Words, 1750–1800*. New York: Thomas Y. Crowell, 1987.

America Is Ready to Fight

On July 6, 1775, less than two months after the battles at Lexington and Concord, the Continental Congress issued its Declaration of Causes of Taking Up Arms. *The document, excerpted here, was intended to show that American patriots had so far explored all peaceful avenues of settling their differences with England and that, although they did not want to fight, they would do so if necessary.*

A Congress of delegates from the United Colonies was assembled at Philadelphia on the fifth day of last September. We resolved again to offer an humble and dutiful petition to the king, and also addressed our fellow-subjects of Great Britain. We have pursued every temperate, every respectful measure: we have even proceeded to break off our commercial intercourse with our fellow-subjects, as the last peaceable admonition that our attachment to no nation upon earth should supplant our attachment to liberty. This, we flattered ourselves, was the ultimate step of the controversy; but subsequent events have shewn how vain was this hope of finding moderation in our enemies. . . .

Fruitless were all the entreaties, arguments, and eloquence of an illustrious band of the most distinguished peers and commoners, who nobly and strenuously asserted the justice of our cause, to stay or even to mitigate the heedless fury with which these accumulated and unexampled outrages were hurried on. Equally fruitless was the interference of the City of London, of Bristol, and many other respectable towns in our favour. Parliament adopted an insidious [evil, corrupt] manoeuvre calculated to divide us, to establish a perpetual auction of taxations where colony should bid against colony, all of them uninformed what ransom would redeem their lives; and thus to extort from us, at the point of the bayonet, the unknown sums that should be sufficient to gratify, if possible to gratify ministerial rapacity [greed], with the miserable indulgence left to us of raising, in our own mode, the prescribed tribute. What terms more rigid and humiliating could have been dictated by remorseless victors to conquered enemies? in our circumstances to accept them would be to deserve them. . . .

Our cause is just. Our union is perfect. Our internal resources are great, and, if necessary, foreign assistance is undoubtedly attainable. We gratefully acknowledge, as signal instances of the Divine favour towards us, that His [God's] Providence would not permit us to be called into this severe controversy until we were grown up to our present strength, had been previously exercised in warlike operations, and possessed of the means of defending ourselves. With hearts fortified with these animating reflections, we most solemnly, before God and the world, *declare*, that exerting the utmost energy of those powers which our beneficent Creator hath graciously bestowed upon us, the arms we have been compelled by our enemies to assume, we will, in defiance of every hazard, with unabating firmness and perseverance, employ for the preservation of our liberties; being with one mind resolved to die freemen, rather then to live slaves.

Samuel Eliot Morison, ed., *Sources and Documents Illustrating the American Revolution, 1764–1788, and the Formation of the Federal Constitution.* Oxford, England: Clarendon Press, 1953.

America Should Become a "Free and Independent State"

In May 1776, the citizens of Malden, Massachusetts, sent the Massachusetts House of Representatives this letter expressing their belief that America should become independent of Great Britain.

Sir—A resolution of the hon. house of representatives, calling upon the several towns in this colony to express their minds in respect to the important question of American independence, is the occasion of our now instructing you. The time was, sir, when we loved the king and the people of Great Britain with an affection truly filial [as a son or daughter would]; we felt ourselves interested in their glory; we shared in their joys and sorrows; we cheerfully poured the fruit of all our labours into the lap of our mother country, and without reluctance expended our blood and our treasure in their cause.

These were our sentiments toward Great Britain while she continued to act the part of a parent state; we felt ourselves happy in our connection with her, nor wished it to be dissolved; but our sentiments are altered, it is now the ardent wish of our soul that America may become a free and independent state.

A sense of unprovoked injuries will arouse the resentment of the most peaceful. Such injuries these colonies have received from Britain. Unjustifiable claims have been made by the king and his minions [subordinates] to tax us without our consent; these claims have been prosecuted in a manner cruel and unjust to the highest degree. The frantic policy of administration hath induced them to send fleets and armies to America; that, by depriving us of our trade, and cutting the throats of our brethren, they might awe us into submission, and erect a system of despotism [a government where the ruler has unlimited power] in America, which should so far enlarge the influence of the crown as to enable it to rivet their shackles upon the people of Great Britain.

This plan was brought to a crisis upon the ever memorable nineteenth of April [1776; battles at Lexington and Concord, Massachusetts]. We remember the fatal day! the expiring groans of our countrymen yet vibrate on our ears! and we now behold the flames of their peaceful dwellings ascending to Heaven! we hear their blood crying to us from the ground for vengeance! charging us, as we value the peace of their names, to have no further connection with —, who can unfeelingly hear of the slaughter of —, and composedly sleep with their blood upon his soul. The manner in which the war has been prosecuted hath confirmed us in these sentiments; piracy and murder, robbery and breach of faith, have been conspicuous [obvious] in the conduct of the king's troops: defenceless towns have been attacked and destroyed: . . . the cries of the widow and the orphan demand our attention; they demand that the hand of pity should wipe the tear from their eye, and that the sword of their country should avenge their wrongs. We long entertained hope that the spirit of the British nation would once more induce them to assert their own and our rights, and bring to condign [deserved] punishment the elevated villains who have trampled upon the sacred rights of men and affronted the majesty of the people. We hoped in vain; they have lost their love to freedom, they have lost their spirit of just resentment; we therefore renounce with disdain our connection with a kingdom of slaves; we bid a final adieu to Britain.

Could an accommodation now be effected, we have reason to think that it would be fatal to the liberties of America; we should soon catch the contagion of venality [corruption] and dissipation [excess], which hath Britains to lawless domination. Were we placed in the situation we were in 1763: were the powers of appointing to offices, and commanding the militia, in the hands of governors, our arts, trade and manufactures, would be cramped; nay, more than this, the life of every man who has been active in the cause of his country would be endangered.

For these reasons, as well as many others which might be produced, we are confirmed in the opinion, that the present age would be deficient in their duty to God, their posterity and themselves, if they do not establish an American republic. This is the only form of government which we wish to see established; for we can never be willingly subject to any other King than he who, being possessed of infinite wisdom, goodness and rectitude [moral integrity], is alone fit to possess unlimited power.

On July 4, 1776, delegates of the second Continental Congress signed the Declaration of Independence.

We have freely spoken our sentiments upon this important subject, but we mean not to dictate; we have unbounded confidence in the wisdom and uprightness of the continental congress: with pleasure we recollect that this affair is under their direction; and we now instruct you, sir, to give them the strongest assurance, that, if they should declare America to be a free and independent republic, your constituents will support and defend the measure, to the last drop of their blood, and the last farthing of their treasure.

Hezekiah Niles, ed., *Principles and Acts of the Revolution in America*. Baltimore, MD: 1822.

The Declaration of Independence

On July 4, 1776, after two days of debate and revision, the delegates at the second Continental Congress signed the Declaration of Independence, the document proclaiming the colonies' right to be free.

WHEN in the Course of human events, it becomes necessary for one people to dissolve the political bands which have connected them with another, and to assume among the Powers of the earth, the separate and equal Station to which the Laws of Nature and of Nature's God entitle them, a decent respect to the opinions of mankind requires that they should declare the causes which impel them to the separation.—We hold these truths to be self-evident, that all men are created equal, that they are endowed by their Creator with certain unalienable Rights, that among these are Life, Liberty, and the pursuit of Happiness.—That to secure these rights, Governments are instituted among Men, deriving their just powers from the consent of the governed.—That whenever any Form of Government becomes destructive of these ends, it is the Right of the People to alter or to abolish it, and to institute new Government, laying its foundation on such principles and organizing its powers in such form, as to them shall seem most likely to effect their Safety and Happiness. Prudence, indeed, will dictate that Governments long established should not be changed for light and transient causes; and accordingly all experience hath shewn, that mankind are more disposed to suffer, while evils are sufferable, than to right themselves by abolishing the forms to which they are accustomed. But when a long train of abuses and usurpations, pursuing invariably the same Object, evinces a design to reduce them under absolute Despotism, it is their right, it is their duty, to throw off such Government, and to provide new Guards for their future security.—Such has been the patient sufferance of these Colonies; and such is now the necessity which constrains them to alter their former System of Government. The history of the present King of Great Britain is a history of repeated injuries and usurpations, all having in direct object the establishment of an absolute Tyranny over these States. To prove this, let the Facts be submitted to a candid world.—He has refused his Assent to Laws, the most wholesome and necessary for the public good.—He has forbidden his Governors to pass Laws of immediate and pressing importance, unless suspended in their operation till his Assent should be obtained; and when so suspended, he has utterly neglected to attend to them.—He has refused to pass other Laws for the accommodation of large districts of people, unless those people would relinquish the right of

Representation in the Legislature, a right inestimable to them and formidable to tyrants only.—He has called together legislative bodies at places unusual, uncomfortable, and distant from the depository of their public Records, for the sole purpose of fatiguing them into compliance with his measures.—He has dissolved Representative Houses repeatedly, for opposing with manly firmness his invasions on the rights of the people.—He has refused for a long time, after such dissolutions, to cause others to be elected; whereby the Legislative powers, incapable of Annihilation, have returned to the People at large for their exercise; the State remaining in the mean time exposed to all the dangers of invasion from without, and convulsions within.—He has endeavored to prevent the population of these States; for that purpose obstructing Laws for naturalization of Foreigners; refusing to pass others to encourage their migrations hither, and raising the conditions of new Appropriations of Lands.— He has obstructed the Administration of Justice, by refusing his Assent to Laws for establishing Judiciary Powers.—He has made Judges dependent on his Will alone, for the tenure of their offices, and the amount and payment of their salaries.—He has erected a multitude of New Offices, and sent hither swarms of Officers to harass our people, and eat out their substance.—He has kept among us, in times of peace, Standing Armies without the Consent of our Legislatures.—He has affected to render the Military independent of and superior to the Civil power.—He has combined with others to subject us to a jurisdiction foreign to our constitution, and unacknowledged by our laws; giving his Assent to their Acts of pretended Legislation:—For quartering large bodies of armed troops among us:—For protecting them by a mock Trial, from punishment for any Murders which they should commit on the Inhabitants of these States:—For cutting off our Trade with all parts of the World:— For imposing Taxes on us without our Consent:—For depriving us in many cases of the benefits of Trial by Jury:—For transporting us beyond Seas to be tried for pretended offenses:—For abolishing the free System of English Laws in a neighboring—Province, establishing therein an Arbitrary government, and enlarging its Boundaries so as to render it at once an example and fit instrument for introducing the same absolute rule into these Colonies:—For taking away our

Charters, abolishing our most valuable Laws, and altering fundamentally the Forms of our Governments:—For suspending our own Legislatures, and declaring themselves invested with power to legislate for us in all cases whatsoever.—He has abdicated Government here, by declaring us out of his Protection and waging war against us.—He has plundered our seas, ravaged our Coasts, burnt our towns, and destroyed the lives of our people.—He is at this time transporting large Armies of foreign Mercenaries to complete the works of death, desolation and tyranny, already begun with circumstances of Cruelty and perfidy [disloyalty] scarcely paralleled in the most barbarous ages, and totally unworthy the Head of a civilized nation.— He has constrained our fellow Citizens taken captive on the high Seas to bear Arms against their Country, to become the executioners of their friends and Brethren, or to fall themselves by their Hands.—He has excited domestic insurrections amongst us, and has endeavored to bring on the inhabitants of our frontiers, the merciless Indian Savages, whose rule of warfare is an undistinguished destruction of all ages, sexes and conditions. In every stage of these Oppressions We have Petitioned for Redress in the most humble terms. Our repeated Petitions have been answered only by repeated injury. A Prince, whose character is thus Marked by every act which may define a Tyrant, is unfit to be the ruler of a free people. —Nor have We been wanting in attentions to our British brethren. We have warned them from time to time of attempts by their legislature to extend an unwarrantable jurisdiction over us. We have reminded them of the circumstances of our emigration and settlement here. We have appealed to their native justice and magnanimity, and we have conjured them by the ties of our common kindred to disavow these usurpations, which would inevitably interrupt our connections and correspondence. They too have been deaf to the voice of justice and of consanguinity [related by blood]. We must, therefore, acquiesce in the necessity which denounces our Separation, and hold them, as we hold the rest of mankind, Enemies in War, in Peace Friends.

WE THEREFORE, the Representatives of the UNITED STATES OF AM-ERICA, in General Congress, Assembled, appealing to the Supreme Judge of the world for the rectitude of our intentions, do, in the Name, and by the authority of the good People of these Colonies, solemnly publish and declare, That these United Colonies are and of Right ought to be FREE AND INDEPENDENT STATES; that they are Absolved from all Allegiance to the British Crown, and that all political connection between them and the State of Great Britain, is and ought to be totally dissolved; and that as Free and Independent States, they have full Power to levy War, conclude Peace, contract Alliances, establish Commerce, and to do all other Acts and Things which Independent States may of right do. And for the support of this Declaration, with a firm reliance on the protection of Divine Providence, We mutually pledge to each other our Lives, our Fortunes, and our sacred Honor.

The Continental Congress, Declaration of Independence, 1776.

The Battle of Long Island

The Battle of Long Island was almost the last for George Washington's army. Forced to retreat during the night of August 29, 1776, Washington ultimately saved his men. Colonel Benjamin Tallmadge, a member of the army, describes the battle and the retreat.

This was the first time in my life that I had witnessed the awful scene of a battle when man was engaged to destroy fellowman. I well remember my sensations on the occasion, for they were solemn beyond description. . . . Our entrenchment was so weak that it is most wonderful the British general did not attempt to storm it soon after the battle in which his troops had been victorious. . . .

It was one of the most anxious, busy nights that I ever recollect, and being the third in which hardly any of us had closed our eyes in sleep, we were all greatly fatigued. As the dawn of the next day approached, those of us who remained in the trenches became very anxious for our own safety, and when the dawn appeared there were several regiments still on duty. At this time a very dense fog began to rise, and it seemed to settle in a peculiar manner over both encampments. I recollect this peculiar providential occurrence perfectly well; and so very dense was the atmosphere that I could scarcely discern a man at six yards' distance.

When the sun rose we had just received orders to leave the lines, but before we reached the ferry, the commander in chief sent one of his aides to order the regiment to repair again to their former station on the lines. Colonel Chester immediately faced to the right about and returned, where we tarried until the sun had risen, but the fog remained as dense as ever. Finally, the second order arrived for the regiment to retire, and we very joyfully bid those trenches a long adieu. When we reached Brooklyn ferry, the boats had not returned from their last trip, but they very soon appeared and took the whole regiment over to New York; and I think I saw General Washington on the ferry stairs when I stepped into one of the last boats that received the troops. I left my horse tied to a post at the ferry.

The troops having now all safely reached New York, and the fog continuing as thick as ever, I began to think of my favorite horse and requested leave of volunteers to go with me, and guiding the boat myself, I obtained my horse and got off some distance into the river before the enemy appeared in Brooklyn.

As soon as they reached the ferry we were saluted merrily from their musketry, and finally by their field pieces; but we returned in safety. In the history of warfare I do not recollect a more fortunate retreat. After all, the providential appearance of the fog saved a part of our army from being captured, and certainly myself, among others who formed the rear guard. General Washington has never received the credit which was due to him for this wise and most fortunate measure.

Milton Meltzer, ed., *The American Revolutionaries: A History in Their Own Words, 1750–1800.* New York: Thomas Y. Crowell, 1987.

Black Enlistment

By 1778, the need for fresh troops led George Washington and the Continental Congress to allow blacks to enlist in the Continental Army. The Rhode Island enlistment bill, excerpted here, laid out the rights and privileges of such enlistment, including a clause that said slaves, upon joining the army, would be freed.

African American recruits answer the call for fresh troops.

It is voted and resolved, that every able-bodied Negro, mulatto, or Indian man slave in this state, may enlist . . . to serve during the continuance of the present war with Great Britain.

That every slave, so enlisting, shall be entitled to, and receive all the bounties, wages, and encouragements, allowed by the Continental Congress, to any soldier enlisting into their service.

It is further voted and resolved, that every slave, so enlisting shall, upon his passing muster before Colonel Christopher Greene, be immediately discharged from the service of his master or mistress, and be absolutely FREE, as though he had never been encumbered with any kind of servitude or slavery.

And in case such slave shall, by sickness or otherwise, be rendered unable to maintain himself, he shall not be chargeable to his master or his mistress; but shall be supported at the expense of the state.

And whereas, slaves have been, by the laws, deemed the property of their owners, and therefore compensation ought to be made to the owners for the loss of their service;

It is further voted and resolved, that there be allowed, and paid by this state, to the owner, for every such slave so enlisting a sum according to his worth; at a price not exceeding £120 for the most valuable slave; and in proportion for a slave of less value.

Milton Meltzer, ed., *The American Revolutionaries: A History in Their Own Words, 1750–1800.* New York: Thomas Y. Crowell, 1987.

"Rascally Stupidity"

Life in the Continental Army was bitter during the winter. With little food and inadequate supplies, George Washington and his men struggled to survive. Most colonists hesitated to help for fear of British discovery and punishment. One American soldier wrote this letter to his brother, pleading for help.

The rascally stupidity which now prevails in the country at large is beyond all descriptions. They patiently see our illustrious commander at the head of twenty-five hundred or three thousand ragged, though virtuous and good, men and be obliged to put up with what no troops ever did before.

Why don't you reinforce your army, feed them, clothe, and pay them? Why do you suffer the enemy to have a foothold on the continent? You can prevent it. Send your men to the field, believe you are Americans, not suffer yourselves to be duped into the thought that the French will relieve you and fight your battles. It is your own superiorness that induced Congress to ask foreign aid. It is a reflection too much for a soldier. You don't deserve to be free men, unless you can believe it yourselves. When they arrive, they will not put up with such treatment as your army have done. They will not serve week after week without meat, without clothing, and paid in filthy rags.

I despise my countrymen. I wish I could say I was not born in America. I once gloried in it, but am now ashamed of it. If you do your duty, though late, you may finish the war this campaign. You must immediately fill your regiments and pay your troops in hard monies. They cannot exist as soldiers otherwise. The insults and neglect which the army have met with from the country beggars all description. It must go no farther; they can endure it no longer. I have wrote in a passion. Indeed, I am scarce ever free from it . . . and all this for my cowardly countrymen who flinch at the very time when their exertions are wanted and hold their purse strings as though they would damn the world rather than part with a dollar to their army.

Milton Meltzer, ed., The American Revolutionaries: *A History in Their Own Words,* *1750–1800.* New York: Thomas Y. Crowell, 1987.

"The Terror of the Punishment"

Army discipline during the Revolutionary War was brutish and violent. Penalties ranged from lashes, to life in prison, to death. The following excerpt is from the testimony of James Thatcher, a surgeon's mate, who witnessed such punishment.

The culprit being securely tied to a tree or post receives on his naked back the number of lashes assigned him, by a whip formed of several small knotted cords, which sometimes cut through the skin at every stroke. However strange it may appear, a soldier will often receive the severest stripe without uttering a groan or once shrieking from the lash, even while the blood flows freely from his lacerated wounds. This must be ascribed to stubbornness or pride. They have, however, adopted a method which they say mitigates the anguish in some measure. It is by putting between the teeth a leaden bullet, on which they chew while under the lash, till it is made quite flat and jagged. In some instances of incorrigible villains, it is adjudged by the court that the culprit receive his punishment at several different times, a certain number of stripes repeated at intervals of two or three days, in which case the wounds are in a state of inflammation and the skin rendered more sensibly tender, and the terror of the punishment is greatly aggravated.

Milton Meltzer, ed., *The American Revolutionaries: A History in Their Own Words, 1750–1800.* New York: Thomas Y. Crowell, 1987.

Prisoners of War

Both American and British prisoners of war endured deplorable conditions. Here, an American officer describes the Pennsylvania prison where he lived for more than six months.

I arrived at the jail in Philadelphia [Pennsylvania] about eight o'clock in the evening. I was locked into a cold room destitute of everything but cold stone walls and bare floors—no kind of a seat to sit on—all total darkness, no water to drink or a morsel to eat; destitute a blanket to cover me, I groped about my solitary cell, and in moving about I found that there were two or three persons lying on the floor asleep. I said nothing to them, nor they to me. I stood on my feet and leaned back against the wall, and sometimes moved about the room, and then to change my position I sat on the floor, but no sleep nor slumber; parched with thirst and no one on which I could call for a drop of water. In short, it was a long, dismal, dreary and most gloomy night that I ever beheld.

I reflected on the miseries of the damn'd in that eternal, friendless prison of despair, but still hope hovered around my soul that I should see another morning. Morning finally arrived, and at a late hour, we were furnished with some very hard sea bread and salted pork, and I was able to obtain some water to drink. Being altogether moneyless I could purchase nothing for my comfort. I pretty soon sold my watch for half its value, and with the money I received for it I was able to procure some food pleasant to my taste. I wholly gave up my allowance of provisions to the poor soldiers.

At this time and in this jail were confined 700 prisoners of war. A few small rooms were sequestered for the officers. Each room must contain sixteen men, we fully covered the whole floor when we lay down to sleep, and the poor soldiers were shut into rooms of the same magnitude with double the number. The poor soldiers were soon seized with the jailfever, as it was called, and it swept off in the course of three months 400 men, who were all buried in one continued grave without coffins. The length of a man was the width of the grave, lying three deep one upon another. I thus lived in jail from the 5th of October 1777, till the month of May 1778. Our number daily decreasing. . . . Such a scene of mortality I never witnessed before. Death was so frequent that it ceased to terrify. It ceased to warn; it ceased to alarm survivors.

Milton Meltzer, ed., *The American Revolutionaries: A History in Their Own Words, 1750–1800*. New York: Thomas Y. Crowell, 1987.

Chapter Five

A New Nation Emerges

W hen the war for independence ended in 1783, the colonists were left with a ravaged country in desperate need of structure and leadership. Nothing made this more apparent than a Massachusetts rebellion, called Shays's Rebellion, in which destitute farmers rose up against the state government. The farmers, unable to pay their debts following a severe economic depression, protested both the state's confiscation of their lands and what they believed was unfair representation in the legislature. General George Washington and others pointed to Shays's Rebellion and called for a strong national government that would, among other things, prevent future insurrections.

Such a government was slow in coming, however. Each of the thirteen colonies had its own ideas about how the government should be structured. In the spring of 1787, delegates from each of the colonies converged upon the city of Philadelphia, Pennsylvania, for a meeting called the Constitutional Convention to draw up a constitution, or set of laws, outlining how the new nation would be run.

One of the more contentious debates during this convention was that of states' versus federal rights. Many delegates worried that a strong federal government would supplant the states, giving them little voice in the maintenance of the nation. Others, however, argued that many of the nation's problems stemmed from the disagreements and bickering between states. A strong national government, these proponents said, would unite the country and allow the thirteen states to work toward common goals. Other issues also divided the convention—among them, slavery and representation in the legislature—but by June 1788, a constitution had been agreed upon, and the delegates from New Hampshire became the first to sign it.

Although the Constitution provided a working set of laws, some people believed there was one notable omission: a bill of rights, outlining the rights afforded to the common people. Such well-known state representatives as Thomas Jefferson and George Mason both voiced strong criticisms of the Constitution as it was. The lack of a bill of rights would endanger the natural freedoms of the American people, they argued. Mason, for one, proposed that states go so far as not to ratify, or approve, the Constitution without a bill of rights.

After the war for independence, angry farmers rose up against the Massachusetts State government in what came to be known as Shays's Rebellion.

Despite that suggestion, ratification proceeded, as did the drafting of a bill of rights. These rights would become the first ten amendments to the Constitution, guaranteeing such privileges as freedom of speech, a free press, and the right to bear arms.

By 1791, George Washington had become the country's first president, and all thirteen states had ratified both the Constitution and the Bill of Rights. The once disparate colonies of the early European settlers had become a single, unified nation.

A Crisis of Authority

On March 16, 1787, the American Recorder, *a Massachusetts newspaper, published an editorial in reaction to Shays's Rebellion. In this excerpt, the paper's editors argue that the event demonstrated the need for a strong national government.*

This [Shays's Rebellion] is a crisis in our affairs, which requires all the wisdom and energy of government; for every man of sense must be convinced that our disturbances have arisen, more from a want of power, than the abuse of it—from the relaxation, and almost annihilation of our federal government—from the feeble, unsystematic, ... inconstant character of our own state—from the derangement of our finances—the oppressive absurdity of our mode of taxation—and from the astonishing enthusiasm and perversion of principles among the people. It is not extraordinary that commotions have been excited. It is strange, that under the circumstances which we have been discussing, that they did not appear sooner, and terminate more fatally. For let it be remarked, that a feeble government produces more factions [dissenting groups] than an oppressive one. The want of power first makes individuals pretended legislators, and then, active rebels. Where parents want authority, children are wanting in duty. It is not possible to advance further in the same path. Here the ways divide, the one will conduct us to anarchy, and next to foreign or domestic tyranny: the other, by the wise and vigorous exertion of lawful authority, will lead to permanent power, and general prosperity. I am no advocate for despotism [dictatorship]; but I believe the probability to be much less of its being introduced by the corruption of our rules, than by the delusion of the people. . . .

While the bands of union are so loose, we are no more entitled to the character of a nation than the hordes of vagabond traitors. Reason has ever condemned our paltry [insignificant] prejudices upon this important subject. Now that experience has come in aid of reason, let us renounce them. For what is there now to prevent our subjugation by a foreign power, but their contempt of the acquisition? It is time to render the federal head supreme in the United States.

William Dudley, ed., *The Creation of the Constitution.* San Diego, CA: Greenhaven Press, 1995.

Madison Questions the Power of the Convention

Even among those convention members who were involved in the writing of the Constitution, views were not always positive. In this letter from James Madison to George Washington, Madison wrote about his concern that the Congress did not have the power to write the new Constitution.

It was first urged that as the new Constitution was more than an Alteration of the Articles of Confederation under which Congress acted, and even subverted these articles altogether, there was a Constitutional impropriety in their taking any positive agency in the work. The answer given was that the Resolution of Congress . . . had recommended the Convention as the best mean of obtaining a firm *national Government;* that as the powers of the convention were defined by their Commissions in nearly the same terms with the powers of Congress given by the Confederation on the subject of alterations, Congress were not more restrained from acceding to the new plan, than the Convention were from proposing it. If the plan was within the powers of the Convention it was within those of Congress; if beyond those powers, the same necessity which justified the Convention would justify Congress; and a failure of Congress to Concur in what was done, would imply either that the convention

Delegates from the newly formed United States meet to draft a constitution.

had done wrong in exceeding their powers, or that the Government proposed was in itself liable to insuperable [overwhelming] objections; that such an inference would be the more natural, as Congress had never scrupled to recommend measures foreign to their constitutional functions, whenever the public good seemed to require it; and had in several instances, particularly in the establishment of the new Western Governments, exercised assumed powers of a very high & delicate nature, under motives infinitely less urgent than the present state of our affairs.

The Debate on the Constitution: Federalist and Antifederalist Speeches, Articles, and Letters During the Struggle over Ratification. New York: The Library of America, 1990.

States' Rights Should Be Supreme

One of the most consequential debates at the Constitutional Convention pitted states' rights supporters against those in favor of a strong centralized government. Although the latter eventually won out, those who supported the rights of the states were widely heard. In this excerpt, "Z" (the pseudonym of an anonymous writer) questions the necessity of usurping state government powers with a new centralized government.

It seems to be generally felt and acknowledged, that the affairs of this country are in a ruinous situation. With vast resources in our hands, we are impoverished by the continual drain of money from us in foreign trade; our navigation is destroyed; our people are in debt and unable to pay; industry is at a stand; our public treaties are violated, and national faith, solemnly plighted to foreigners and to our own citizens, is no longer kept. We are discontented at home, and abroad we are insulted and despised.

In this exigency [crisis] people naturally look up to the continental Convention, in hopes that their wisdom will provide some effectual remedy for this complication of disorders. It is perhaps the last opportunity which may be presented to us of establishing a permanent system of Continental Government; and, if this opportunity be lost, it is much to be feared that we shall fall into irretrievable confusion.

How the great object of their meeting is to be attained is a question which deserves to be seriously considered. Some men, there is reason to believe, have indulged the idea of reforming the United States by means of some refined and complicated schemes of organizing a future Congress in a different form. These schemes, like many others with which we have been amused in times past, will be found to be merely visionary, and produce no lasting benefit. The error is not in the form of Congress, the mode of election, or the duration of the appointment of the members. The source of all our misfortunes is evidently in the want of power in Congress. To be convinced of this, we need only recollect the vigor, the energy, the unanimity of this country a few years past, even in the midst of a bloody war, *when Congress governed the continent.* We have gradually declined into feebleness, anarchy and wretchedness, from that period in which the several States began to exercise the sovereign and absolute right of treating the recommendations of Congress with contempt. From that time to the present, we have seen the great Federal Head of our union clothed with the authority of making treaties without the power of performing them; of contracting debts without being able to discharge them, or to bind others to discharge them; of regulating our trade, and providing for the general welfare of the people, in their concerns with foreign nations, without the power of restraining a single individual from the infraction of their orders, or restricting any trade, however injurious to the public welfare.

To remedy these evils, some have weakly imagined that it is necessary to annihilate the several States, and vest Congress with the absolute direction and government of the continent, as one single republic. This, however, would be impracticable and mischievous. In so extensive a country many local and internal regulations would be required, which Congress could not possibly attend to, and to which the States individually are fully competent; but those things which alike concern all the States, such as our foreign trade and foreign transactions, Congress should be fully authorized to regulate, and should be invested with the power of enforcing their regulations.

The ocean, which joins us to other nations, would seem to be the scene upon which Congress might exert its authority with the greatest benefit to the United States, as no one State can possibly claim any exclusive right in it. It has been long seen that the States individually cannot, with any success, pretend to regulate trade. The duties and restrictions which one State imposes, the neighboring States enable the merchants to elude; and besides, if they could be enforced, it would be highly unjust, that the duties collected in the port of one State should be applied to the sole use of that State in which they are collected, whilst the neighboring States, who have no ports for foreign commerce, consume a part of the goods imported, and thus in effect pay a part of the duties. Even if the recommendation of Congress had been attended to, which proposed the levying for the use of Congress five per centum [percent] on goods imported, to be collected by officers to be appointed by the individual States, it is more than probable that the laws would have been feebly executed. Men are not apt to be sufficiently attentive to the business of those who do not appoint, and cannot remove or control them; officers would naturally look up to the State which appointed them, and it is past a doubt that some of the States would esteem it no unpardonable sin to promote their own particular interest, or even that of particular men, to the injury of the United States.

Would it not then be right to vest Congress with the sole and exclusive power of regulating trade, of imposing port duties, of appointing officers to collect these duties, of erecting ports and deciding all questions by their own authority, which concern foreign trade and navigation upon the high seas? Some of those persons, who have conceived a narrow jealousy of Congress, and therefore have unhappily obstructed their exertions for the public welfare, may perhaps be startled at the idea, and make objections. To such I would answer, that our situation appears to be sufficiently desperate to justify the hazarding an experiment of anything which promises immediate relief. Let us try this for a few years; and if we find it attended with mischief, we can refuse to renew the power. But it appears to me to be necessary and useful; and I cannot think that it would in the least degree endanger our liberties. The representatives of the States in Congress are easily changed as often as we please, and they must necessarily be changed often. They would have little inclination and less ability to enterprise against the liberties of their constituents. This, no doubt, would induce the necessity of employing a small number of armed vessels to enforce the regulations of Congress, and would be the beginning of a Continental Navy; but a navy was never esteemed, like a standing army, dangerous to the liberty of the people.

To those who should object that this is too small a power to grant to Congress; that many more are necessary to be added to those which they already possess, I can only say, that perhaps they have not sufficiently reflected upon the great importance of the power proposed. That it would be of immense service to the country I have no doubt, as it is the only means by which our trade can be put on a footing with other nations; that it would in the event greatly strengthen the hands of Congress, I think is highly probable.

"Z," *Freeman's Journal*, May 16, 1787, Philadelphia.

Separation of Powers

As delegates debated in Philadelphia, three members of the Continental Congress—Alexander Hamilton, John Jay, and James Madison drafted the Federalist Papers, a series of eighty-five essays supporting and explaining the Constitution. In this excerpt from Federalist #51, *Madison defends the principle of separation of powers.*

[T]he great security against a gradual concentration of the several powers in the same department consists in giving to those who administer each department the necessary constitutional means and personal motives to resist encroachments of the others. The provision for defense must in this, as in all other cases, be made commensurate to the danger of attack. Ambition must be made to counteract ambition. The interest of the man must be connected with the constitutional rights of the place.

It may be a reflection on human nature that such devices should be necessary to control the abuses of government. But what is government itself but the greatest of all reflections on human nature? If men were angels, no government would be necessary. If angels were to govern men, neither external nor internal controls on government would be necessary. In framing a government which is to be administered by men over men, the great difficulty lies in this: you must first enable the government to control the governed; and in the next place oblige it to control itself. A dependence on the people is, no doubt, the primary control on the government; but experience has taught mankind the necessity of auxiliary [additional] precautions.

Alexander Hamilton, John Jay, and James Madison, *The Federalist Papers.* New York: Bantam Books, 1982.

Judicial Review

In this excerpt from Federalist #78, *Alexander Hamilton defends the doctrine of judicial review, the provision that allows justices to annul legislation or executive acts they find to be unconstitutional.*

The complete independence of the courts of justice is peculiarly essential in a limited constitution. By a limited constitution, I understand one which contains certain specified exceptions to the legislative authority; such, for instance, as that it shall pass no bills of attainder, no *ex post facto* [resulting after the fact] laws, and the like. Limitations of this kind can be preserved in practice no other way than through the medium of courts of justice, whose duty it must be to declare all acts contrary to the manifest tenor of the constitution void. Without this, all the reservations of particular rights or privileges would amount to nothing. . . .

The interpretation of the laws is the proper and peculiar province of the courts. A constitution is, in fact, and must be regarded by the judges as, a fundamental law. It therefore belongs to them to ascertain its meaning as well as the meaning of any particular act proceeding from the legislative body. If there should happen to be an irreconcilable variance between the two, that which has the superior obligations and validity ought, of course, to be preferred; or, in other words, the Constitution ought to be preferred to the statute, the intention of the people to the intention of their agents.

Alexander Hamilton, John Jay, and James Madison, *The Federalist Papers.* New York: Bantam Books, 1982.

In Jefferson's Opinion

Throughout the Constitutional Convention, Thomas Jefferson, who was serving in Paris as ambassador to France, corresponded with a number of the delegates. In a letter written to James Madison on December 20, 1787, Jefferson gives his reactions to the Constitution, highlighting the elements he believes to be particularly beneficial but lamenting the lack of a bill of rights.

I like much the general idea of framing a government which should go on itself peaceably, without needing continual recurrence to the state legislatures. I like the organization of the government into Legislative, Judiciary & Executive. I like the power given to the Legislature to levy taxes; and for that reason solely approve of the greater house [of Congress] being chosen by the people directly. For tho' I think a house chosen by them will be very illy qualified to legislate for the Union, for foreign nations etc., yet this evil does not weigh against the good of preserving inviolate the fundamental principle that people are not to be taxed but by the representatives chosen immediately by themselves. I am captivated by the compromise of the opposite claims of the great & little states, of the latter to equal, and former to proportional influence. I am much pleased too with the substitution of the method of voting by persons, instead of that of voting by states, and I like the negative given to the Executive with a third of either house, though I should have liked it better had the Judiciary been associated for that purpose, or invested with a similar and separate power. . . .

I will now add what I do not like. First the omission of a bill of rights providing clearly . . . for freedom of religion, freedom of the press, protection against standing armies, restriction against monopolies, the eternal and unremitting force of the habeas corpus laws [laws protecting people from illegal imprisonment] and trials by jury in all matters of fact triable by the laws of the land and not by the law of nations. . . .

The second feature I dislike, and greatly dislike, is the abandonment in every instance of the necessity of rotation in office and most particularly in the case of the president. Experience concurs with reason in concluding that the first magistrate will always be re-elected if the Constitution permits it. He is then an officer for life. . . .

I own I am not a friend to a very energetic government. It is always oppressive. The late rebellion in Massachusetts [Shays's Rebellion] has given more alarm than I think it should have done. . . . No country should be so long without [a rebellion]. Nor will any degree of power in the hands of government prevent insurrections.

Thomas Jefferson, *Writings*. New York: Library of America, 1984.

"There Is No Alternative"

George Washington lobbied strongly for the ratification of the Constitution. In this excerpt from a letter written in December 1787, he explains that the Constitution is necessary because its only alternative is anarchy.

My decided opinion on the matter is, that there is no alternative between the adoption of it [the Constitution] and anarchy. . . . All the opposition to it that I have yet seen is addressed more to the passions than to reason. General government is now suspended by a thread; I might go further and say it is really at an end. . . .

The Constitution that is submitted, is not free from imperfections; but there are as few radical defects in it as could well be expected, considering the heterogeneous [mixed] mass of which the Convention was composed—and the diversity of interests which were to be reconciled. A Constitutional door being opened, for future alterations and amendments, I think it would be wise in the People to adopt what is offered to them; and I wish it may be by as great a majority of them as in the body that decided on it.

Jim R. McClellan, *Historical Moments: Changing Interpretations of America's Past: Volume I, the Pre-Colonial Period Through the Civil War*. Guilford, CT: Dushkin Publishing, 1994.

A List of Objections

As the states held individual conventions to ratify the Constitution, some Americans criticized the document, debating what it said and lamenting what it did not say. In this excerpt, a former officer of the Continental Army lists his objections.

To the Citizens of Philadelphia.
Friends, Countrymen, Brethren and Fellow Citizens,
The important day is drawing near when you are to elect delegates to represent you in a Convention, on the result of whose deliberations will depend, in a great measure, your future happiness.

This convention is to determine whether or not the commonwealth of Pennsylvania shall adopt the plan of government proposed by the late convention of delegates from the different states, which sat in this city.

With a heart full of anxiety for the preservation of your dearest rights, I presume to address you on this important occasion—In the name of sacred liberty, dearer to us than our property and our lives, I request your most earnest attention.

The proposed plan of continental government is now fully known to you. You have read it I trust with the attention it deserves—You have heard the objections that have been made to it—You have heard the answers to these objections.

If you have attended to the whole with candor and unbiassed minds, as becomes men that are possessed and deserving of freedom, you must have been alarmed at the result of your observations. Notwithstanding the splendor of names which has attended the publication of the new constitution, notwithstanding the sophistry and vain reasonings that have been urged to support its principles; alas! you must at least have concluded that great men are not always infallible, and that patriotism itself may be led into essential errors.

Objections to the Constitution

The objections that have been made to the new constitution, are these:

1. It is not merely (as it ought to be) a CONFEDERATION of STATES, but a GOVERNMENT of INDIVIDUALS.

2. The powers of Congress extend to the *lives*, the *liberties* and the *property* of every citizen.

3. The *sovereignty* of the different states is *ipso facto* [by the very fact] destroyed in its most essential parts.

4. What remains of it will only tend to create violent dissentions between the state governments and the Congress, and terminate in the ruin of the one or the other.

5. The consequence must therefore be, either that the *union* of the states will be destroyed by a violent struggle, or that their sovereignty will be swallowed up by silent encroachments into a universal aristocracy; because it is clear, that if two different *sovereign powers* have a co-equal command over the *purses* of the citizens, they will struggle for the spoils, and the weakest will be in the end obliged to yield to the efforts of the strongest.

6. Congress being possessed of these immense powers, the liberties of the states and of the people are not secured by a bill or DECLARATION OF RIGHTS.

7. The sovereignty of the states is not expressly reserved, the *form* only, and not the SUBSTANCE of their government, is guaranteed to them by express words.

8. TRIAL BY JURY, that sacred bulwark of liberty, is ABOLISHED IN CIVIL CASES, and Mr. W— (James Wilson), one of the convention, has told you, that not being able to agree as to the FORM of establishing this point, they have left you deprived of the

SUBSTANCE. Here are his own words—*The subject was involved in difficulties. The convention found the task* TOO DIFFICULT *for them, and left the business as it stands.*

9. THE LIBERTY OF THE PRESS is not secured, and the powers of congress are fully adequate to its destruction, as they are to have the trial of *libels*, or *pretended libels* against the United States, and may by a cursed abominable STAMP ACT (as the *Bowdoin administration* has done in Massachusetts) preclude you effectually from all means of information. *Mr. W—has given you no answer to these arguments.*

10. Congress have the power of keeping up a STANDING ARMY in time of peace, and Mr. W—has told you THAT IT WAS NECESSARY.

11. The LEGISLATIVE and EXECUTIVE powers are not kept separate as every one of the American constitutions declares they ought to be; but they are mixed in a manner entirely novel and unknown, even to the constitution of Great Britain; because,

12. In England the king only, has a *nominal negative* over the proceedings of the legislature, which he has NEVER DARED TO EXERCISE since the days of *King William*, whereas by the new constitution, both the *president general* and the *senate* TWO EXECUTIVE BRANCHES OF GOVERNMENT, have that negative, and are intended to *support* each other in the exercise of it.

Problems with Congress

13. The representation of the lower house [the House of Representatives] is too small, consisting only of 65 members.

14. That of the *senate* is so small that it renders its extensive powers extremely dangerous: it is to consist only of 26 members, two-thirds of whom must concur to conclude any *treaty or alliance* with foreign powers: Now we will suppose that five of them are absent, sick, dead, or unable to attend, *twenty-one* will remain, and eight of these (*one-third*, and *one* over) may prevent the conclusion of any treaty, even the most favorable to America. Here will be a fine field for the intrigues and even the *bribery* and *corruption* of European powers.

15. The most important branches of the EXECUTIVE DEPARTMENT are to be put into the hands of a *single magistrate*, who will be in fact an ELECTIVE KING. The MILITARY, the land and naval forces are to be entirely at his disposal, and therefore:

16. Should the *senate*, by the intrigues of foreign powers, become devoted to foreign influence, as was the case of late in *Sweden*, the people will be obliged, as the *Swedes* have been, to seek their refuge in the arms of the *monarch* or PRESIDENT GENERAL.

17. ROTATION, that noble prerogative of liberty, is entirely excluded from the new system of government, and great men may and probably will be continued in office during their lives.

18. ANNUAL ELECTIONS are abolished, and the people are not to re-assume their rights until the expiration of *two, four* and *six* years.

19. Congress are to have the power of fixing the *time, place* and *manner* of holding elections, so as to keep them forever subjected to their influence.

20. The importation of slaves is not to be prohibited until the year 1808, and SLAVERY will probably resume its empire in Pennsylvania.

21. The MILITIA is to be under the immediate command of congress, and men *conscientiously scrupulous of bearing arms*, may be compelled to perform military duty.

22. The new government will be EXPENSIVE beyond any we have ever experienced, the *judicial* department alone, with its concomitant train of *judges, justices, chancellors, clerks, sheriffs, coroners, escheators, state attornies and solicitors, constables, &* in every state and in every county in each state, will be a burden beyond the utmost abilities of the people to bear, and upon the whole:

23. A government partaking of MONARCHY and aristocracy will be fully and firmly established, and liberty will be but a name to adorn the *short* historic page of the halcyon [peaceful] days of America.

These, my countrymen, are the objections that have been made to the new proposed system of government.

An Officer of the Late Continental Army, a letter "To the Citizens of Philadelphia," *Independent Gazetteer*, November 6, 1787, Philadelphia.

Reactions to the Constitution

Americans' reactions to the U.S. Constitution were varied. This anonymous author, called "Brutus," expressed his doubts that a nation as vast as the United States could be governed as a republic.

History furnishes no example of a free republic, any thing like the extent of the United States. The Grecian republics were of small extent; so also was that of the Romans. Both of these, it is true, in process of time, extended their conquests over large territories of country; and the consequence was, that their governments were changed from that of free governments to those of the most tyrannical that ever existed in the world.

Not only the opinion of the greatest men, and the experience of mankind, are against the idea of an extensive republic, but a variety of reasons may be drawn from the reason and nature of things, against it. In every government [one in which the ruler has absolute authority], the will of the sovereign is the law. In despotic governments, the supreme authority being lodged in one, his will is law, and can be as easily expressed to a large extensive territory as to a small one. In a pure democracy the people are the sovereign, and their will is declared by themselves; for this purpose they must all come together to deliberate, and decide. This kind of government cannot be exercised, therefore, over a country of any considerable extent; it must be confined to a single city, or at least limited to such bounds as that the people can conveniently assemble, be able to debate, understand the subject submitted to them, and declare their opinion concerning it.

In a free republic, although all laws are derived from the consent of the people, yet the people do not declare their consent by themselves in person, but by representatives, chosen by them, who are supposed to know the minds of their constituents, and to be possessed of integrity to declare this mind.

In every free government, the people must give their assent to the laws by which they are governed. This is the true criterion between a free government and an arbitrary one. The former are ruled by the will of the whole, expressed in any manner they may agree upon; the latter by the will of one, or a few. If the people are to give their assent to the laws, by persons chosen and appointed by them, the manner of the choice and the number chosen, must be such, as to possess, be disposed, and consequently qualified to declare the sentiments of the people; for if they do not know, or are not disposed to speak the sentiments of the people, the people do not govern, but the sovereignty is in a few. Now, in a large extended country, it is impossible to have a representation, possessing the sentiments, and of integrity, to declare the minds of the people, without having it so numerous and unwieldy, as to be subject in great measure to the inconveniency of a democratic government.

The territory of the United States is of vast extent; it now contains near three millions of souls, and is capable of containing much more than ten times that number. Is it practicable for a country, so large and so numerous as they will soon become, to elect a representation, that will speak their sentiments, without their becoming so numerous as to be incapable of transacting business? It certainly is not.

In a republic, the manners, sentiments, and interests of the people should be similar. If this be not the case, there will be a constant clashing of opinions; and the representatives of one part will be continually striving against those of the other. This will retard the operations of government, and prevent such conclusions as will promote the public good. If we apply this remark to the condition of the United States, we shall be convinced that it forbids that we should be one government. The United States includes a variety of climates. The productions of the different parts of the union are very variant, and their interests, of consequence, diverse. Their manners and habits differ as much as their climates and productions; and their sentiments are by no means coincident. The laws and customs of the several states are, in many respects, very diverse, and in some opposite; each would be in favor of its own interests and customs, and, of consequence, a legislature, formed of representatives from the respective parts, would not only be too numerous to act with any care or decision, but would be composed of such heterogenous and discordant principles, as would constantly be contending with each other.

The laws cannot be executed in a republic, of an extent equal to that of the United States, with promptitude.

The magistrates in every government must be supported in the execution of the laws, either by an armed force, maintained at the public expence for that purpose; or by the people turning out to aid the magistrate upon his command, in case of resistance.

Ralph Ketcham, ed., *The Antifederalist Papers and the Constitutional Convention Debates.* New York: New American Library, 1986.

The Bill of Rights

In 1791, the states ratified the Bill of Rights, authored principally by delegates James Madison and George Mason.

Amendment I

Congress shall make no law respecting an establishment of religion, or prohibiting the free exercise thereof; or abridging the freedom of speech, or of the press; or the right of the people peaceably to assemble, and to petition the Government for a redress of grievances.

Amendment II

A well regulated Militia, being necessary to the security of a free State, the right of the people to keep and bear Arms, shall not be infringed.

Amendment III

No Soldier shall, in time of peace be quartered in any house, without the consent of the Owner, nor in time of war, but in a manner to be prescribed by law.

Amendment IV

The right of the people to be secure in their persons, houses, papers, and effects, against unreasonable searches and seizures, shall not be violated, and no Warrants shall issue, but upon probable cause, supported by Oath or affirmation, and particularly describing the place to be searched, and the persons or things to be seized.

Amendment V

No person shall be held to answer for a capital, or otherwise infamous crime, unless on a presentment or indictment of a Grand Jury, except in cases arising in the land or naval forces, or in the

Militia, when in actual service in time of War or public danger; nor shall any person be subject for the same offence to be twice put in jeopardy of life or limb; nor shall be compelled in any criminal case to be a witness against himself, nor be deprived of life, liberty, or property, without due process of law; nor shall private property be taken for public use, without just compensation.

Amendment VI

In all criminal prosecutions, the accused shall enjoy the right to a speedy and public trial, by an impartial jury of the State and district wherein the crime shall have been committed, which district shall have been previously ascertained by law, and to be informed of the nature and cause of the accusation; to be confronted with the witnesses against him; to have compulsory process for obtaining witnesses in his favor, and to have the Assistance of Counsel for his defence.

Amendment VII

In Suits at common law, where the value in controversy shall exceed twenty dollars, the right of trial by jury shall be preserved, and no fact tried by a jury, shall be otherwise re-examined in any Court of the United States, than according to the rules of the common law.

Amendment VIII

Excessive bail shall not be required, nor excessive fines imposed, nor cruel and unusual punishments inflicted.

Amendment IX

The enumeration in the Constitution, of certain rights, shall not be construed to deny or disparage others retained by the people.

Amendment X

The powers not delegated to the United States by the Constitution, nor prohibited by it to the States, are reserved to the States respectively, or to the people.

William Dudley, ed., *The Creation of the Constitution: Opposing Viewpoints.* San Diego, CA: Greenhaven Press, 1995.

Index

Index